A Treatise on the Blood of Christ

BUT FOR THE
BLOOD

A Treatise on the Blood of Christ

BUT FOR THE
BLOOD

By
David William Koster

ISBN# 978-1-61119-030-4

Printed in the United States of America.

Printed by Calvary Publishing
A Ministry of Parker Memorial Baptist Church
1902 East Cavanaugh Road
Lansing, Michigan 48910
www.CalvaryPublishing.org

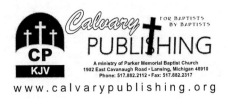

Calvary PUBLISHING
FOR BAPTISTS BY BAPTISTS
CP KJV
A ministry of Parker Memorial Baptist Church
1902 East Cavanaugh Road • Lansing, Michigan 48910
Phone: 517.882.2112 • Fax: 517.882.2317
www.calvarypublishing.org

<u>Acknowledgements</u>

I would like to thank the faithful few who have yielded to the call to preach, forsook the riches of this world and have carried on the old time independent, fundamental, Authorized 1611 King James Bible preaching Baptist Ministry. Without these preachers of the true Word of God this soul would still be on its way to Hell.

I would also like to thank my wife for her strong belief in the Bible and for her support of my Bible studies.

D.W.K.

<u>Foreword</u>

But for the blood, who can complete the thought with a dry eye? But for the blood, who can complete the sentence without falling on one's knees and thanking God for His mercy and grace? But for the blood, how could we ever attain victory over death and the grave? But for the blood that Jesus shed on Mt. Calvary, we would be, of all men, most miserable because without the shedding of His blood there would be no remission of our sins.

This treatise will attempt to demonstrate the Biblical truth that only the sinless blood of our Lord and Saviour, Jesus Christ, can atone for sin and save one's soul from an eternity of suffering in the lake which burneth with fire and brimstone. The 1611 Authorized King James Bible is used exclusively because, **"The words of the LORD *are* pure words: *as* silver tried in a furnace of earth, purified seven times."** (Psm 12:6) and **"All scripture is given by inspiration of God, and *is* profitable for doctrine, for reproof, for correction, and for instruction in righteousness: That the man of God may be perfect, thoroughly furnished unto all good works."** (2 Tim 3:16-17).

Background

The American Heart Association rightly calls blood *the gift of life*, for without blood one would not have life. Historically blood has been inextricable from religion. Anthropological examinations of world cultures provides clear evidence that blood has had, and still has today, special symbolic significance in religious rites. Liquid substances used in sacrificial ceremonies, such as wine, honey, milk, and special concoctions are in almost all cases symbolical substitutes for blood. People still use animal blood and "sacred" potions in religious ceremonies even today in a vain attempt to make peace with their god.

Human blood has been the sacrificial medium of choice because it represents the ultimate sacrifice, another human life. Almost all cultures at one point or another believed that human blood would appease their angry god and would, in one way or another, ward off divine chastisement.

These unfortunates fail to realize or refuse to acknowledge that there is only one true God. The Bible makes it perfectly clear that the one and only true God is the God presented to man in the King James Bible; **"Thus saith the LORD the King of Israel, and his redeemer the LORD of hosts; I *am* the first, and I *am* the last; and beside me *there is* no God. And who, as I, shall call, and shall declare it, and set it in order for me, since I appointed the ancient people? And the things that are coming, and shall come, let them shew unto them." (Is 44:6-7). "... Is there a God beside me? yea, *there is* no God; I know not *any*." (Is 44:8). "Thus saith the LORD, thy redeemer, and he that** formed thee from the womb, I *am* the **LORD** that maketh all *things*; that stretcheth forth the heavens alone; that spreadeth abroad the earth by myself; That frustrateth the tokens of the liars, and maketh diviners mad; that turneth wise *men* backward, and maketh their knowledge foolish; That confirmeth the word of his messengers [the prophets that wrote the Bible]; ..."** (Isa 44:24-25).

And for all the vain sacrifices made since time immemorial, one should note that in actuality, the LORD has not accepted one of them because He said; **"I will have mercy, and not sacrifice: for I am not come to call the righteous, but sinners to repentance."** (Matt 9:13). God would much prefer that all present their bodies as a living sacrifice than to perform vain human sacrifices and religious rituals because; **"To do justice and judgement is more acceptable to the LORD than sacrifice."** (Prov 21:3). God points out that; **"Their idols *are* silver and gold, the work of men's hands. They have mouths, but they speak not: eyes have they, but they see not: They have ears, but they hear not: noses have they, but they smell not: They have hands, but they handle not: feet have they, but they walk not: neither speak they through their throat. ..."**(Psm 115:4-7). God came because; **"... They that make them are like unto them; *so is* every one that trusteth in them."** (Psm 115:8). God did not come to condemn the world but to save it. **"For God sent not his Son into the world to condemn the world; but that the world through him might be saved."** (Jn 3:17). If only all those who are enslaved to religion and customs realized that; **"... if thou seek him, he will be found of** thee, ..." (1 Chron 28:9) "...(for thou [the LORD], *even* thou only, knowest the hearts of all the children of men;)" (1 Kings 8:39). "... the LORD searcheth all hearts, and understandeth all the imaginations of the thoughts:" (1 Chron 28:9).

God's Creation

Genesis 1:1 informs us that God created the heaven and earth and all that is in them in six days; "**In the beginning God created the heaven and the earth. And the earth was without form, and void: and darkness was upon the face of the deep. And the spirit of God moved upon the face of the waters.**"

John 1:1-3 re-affirms this truth; "**In the beginning was the Word, and the Word was with God, and the Word was God. The same was in the beginning with God. All things were made by him; and without him was not any thing made that was made.**" as does John 1:10; "**He [Jesus] was in the world, and world was made by him, and the world knew him not.**"

Along with the creation of heaven and earth, God also established laws of operation for every aspect of His creation. We know these laws as the laws of physical science. They govern the physical world we live in, (e.g. the laws of thermodynamics). In fact, all the "achievements" of man are due to mans ability to creatively exploit these physical laws. Millions of people throughout history have dedicated their lives to the discernment and understanding of these laws. We refer to these fields of endeavor as Science and Engineering.

A Living Soul

Genesis 2:7 informs us that: **"God created man in his own image, in the image of God created he him; male and female created he them."** **"And the LORD God formed man of the dust of the ground, and breathed into his nostrils the breath of life; and man became a living soul."** (Gen 1:27).

The precious breath of life breathed into Adam by God Himself made man a living soul. However, one should realize that as a living soul you do not have autonomy. You belong to God, your creator. Ezekiel 18:3-4 emphatically makes this point; *"As* **I live, saith the Lord God, ... all souls are mine; as the soul of the father, so also the soul of the son is mine: the soul that sinneth, it shall die."** God is the undisputed owner of your soul and He has every right to expect strict obedience. God expects each and every person to obey His Word (the King James Bible) because it **"...** *is* **profitable for doctrine, for reproof, for correction, and for instruction in righteousness: That the man of God may be perfect, thoroughly furnished unto all good works."** (2 Tim 3:16-17). Conversely, disobedient souls have **"But a certain fearful looking for of judgment and fiery indignation ..."** (Heb 10:27). So for anyone who might think they are their own man remember **"... God** *is* **King of all the earth ..."** (Psm 47:7) and He commands all to **"Sanctify yourselves therefore, and be ye holy: for I** *am* **the LORD your God. And ye shall keep my statutes, and do them: I** *am* **the LORD which sanctify you."** (Lev 20:7-8). The bottom line is, man is to **"... Fear God, and keep his commandments: for this is the whole** *duty* **of man."** (Ecc 12:13).

The Flesh

Job confirms that life is a gift; **"Thou hast granted me life and favour, and thy visitation hath preserved my spirit."** (Job 10:12) for **"The spirit of God hath made me, and the breath of the Almighty hath given me life."** (Job 33:4).

Job also informs us that the soul presides over the flesh because he states that God **"... hast clothed me [the soul] with skin and flesh, and hast fenced me with bones and sinews."** (Job 10:11). The body God clothed man's soul with is a very complex and intricate creation in its own right, and is composed of approximately 100 trillion cells. Each cell must be individually tended to, to sustain life. The care and nourishment of the body's cells is performed by the blood. Hence the Biblical truth, the life of the flesh is in the blood.

Thus it is clear that life cometh only from God and because life is in the blood, the Levitical Law prohibits the eating of blood; **"Moreover ye shall eat no manner of blood, whether it be of fowl or of beast, in any of your dwellings. Whatsoever soul it be that eateth any manner of blood, even that soul shall be cut off from his people."** (Lev 7:26-27). Contrary to the beliefs of savages and cannibals, a person cannot receive an animal's power or a person's prowess by the consumption of their blood. Life is a God given gift that cannot be transferred. **"For it is the life of all flesh; the blood of it is for the life thereof: therefore I said unto the children of Israel, Ye shall eat the blood of no manner of flesh: for the life of all flesh is the blood thereof: whosoever eateth it shall be cut off."** (Lev 17:14).

Blood is sacred to God and trying to gain life attributes through the blood of an animal is a serious matter and God provides a severe warning against its consumption; **"Only be sure that thou eat not the blood: for the blood is the life; and thou mayest not eat the life with the flesh. Thou shalt not eat it; thou shalt pour it upon the earth as water. Thou shalt not eat it; that it may go well with thee, and with thy children after thee, when thou shalt do that which is right in the sight of the LORD."** (Deut 12:23-25).

However, if people do not heed this warning and eat blood, they will become idol worshipers and participate in other abominations with righteous judgment to follow; **"Thus saith the Lord GOD; Ye eat with the blood, and lift up your eyes toward your idols, and shed blood: and shall ye possess the land? ... Thus saith the Lord GOD; As I live, surely they that are in the wastes shall fall by the sword, and him that is in the open field will give to the beasts to be devoured, and they that be in the forts and in the caves shall die of the pestilence. ...Then shall they know that I am the LORD, when I have laid the land most desolate because of all their abominations which they have committed."** (Ezek 33:25, 27, 29).

Cardiovascular System
God **"... breathed into his [Adam's] nostrils the breath of life; and man became a living soul."** (Gen 2:7). God oxygenated Adam's red blood cells and started his circulatory system thereby providing the breath of life via the blood to every cell in his body.

Man has what is defined as a closed circulatory

system which is normally referred to as the cardiovascular system. Closed circulatory systems have the blood contained at all times within vessels of different size and wall thickness. Mans cardiovascular system includes a heart, which is a muscular pump that contracts to propel blood out to the body through arteries, and blood vessels.

Arteries are blood vessels that carry blood away from the heart. Arterial walls are able to expand and contract. Arteries have three layers of thick walls. Smooth muscle fibers contract, another layer of connective tissue is quite elastic, allowing the arteries to carry blood under high pressure. Arteries branch into arterioles which in turn branch into collections of capillaries known as capillary beds.

Capillaries are microscopic, one cell thick, blood vessels that act as the point of interchange between the blood and the cells. Blood flow into capillary beds is controlled by nerve-controlled sphincters. It is in the capillary beds that the blood's oxygen, nutrients, and hormones pass into the cells. Likewise, cell waste products, such as carbon dioxide and ammonia pass into the blood for removal and eventual elimination from the body. It is estimated that the human body contains between 50,000 and 60,000 miles of capillaries.

Blood leaving the capillary beds flow into progressively larger venules that in turn join to form veins, which in turn return the blood to the heart. The blood pressure in the veins is low and so veins are constructed with integral valves to prevent the back-flow of blood. Muscular contractions move the blood along.

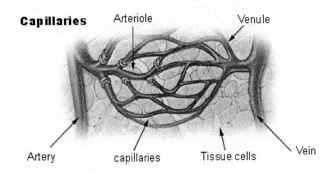

Capillaries   Arteriole   Venule

Artery   capillaries   Tissue cells   Vein

<u>Blood</u>

The circulating fluid in the cardiovascular system is referred to as blood, and the life of the flesh (body's cells) is in the blood. This is why the medical profession characterizes blood as connective tissue.

As stated previously, blood is the fluid that transports nutrients and oxygen to every cell in the body. It also transports wastes away from cells. In an average healthy adult, the volume of blood in milliliters is approximately 8% of the body weight in grams, or about 5 liters (1.3 gallons). Our blood is created in the marrow of the long bones. Blood helps regulate body temperature by carrying excess heat from inner regions of the body to the skin where it can be dissipated, it also fights infection and carries chemicals that regulate many of the body's functions.

Blood is several times thicker than water, 1 pint of which, weighs approximately 1 pound. The red blood cells give blood its overall red in color. Arterial blood is bright red due to its high oxygen content. Venous blood on the other hand is a darker, dull red due to the fact that it has given up much of its oxygen to the cells it services.

Red Blood Cells

Red cells are relatively large microscopic cells without nuclei, approximately 7 microns in diameter. Red cells normally make up 39% of the total blood volume. They transport oxygen from the lungs to all of the living tissues of the body and carry away carbon dioxide. Red cells are produced continually in our bone marrow from stem cells. Hemoglobin is the gas transporting protein molecule that makes up 95% of a red cell. Each red cell has about 270 million iron-rich hemoglobin molecules. Red blood cells remain viable for only about four months after which they are removed from the blood and their components recycled in the spleen. A cubic millimeter of human blood contains about 5 million red blood cells.

White Blood Cells

White blood cells exist in variable numbers and types and make up only about 1% of the blood's volume. Certain white blood cells (lymphocytes) are the first responders for our immune system. They seek out, identify, and bind to the alien protein on bacteria, viruses, and fungi. Other white blood cells (granulocytes and macrophages) then arrive to surround and destroy the foreign matter. Individual white blood cells usually only last 18-36 hours before they also are removed, though some types live as much as a year. A cubic millimeter of human blood contains about 5-10 thousand white blood cells.

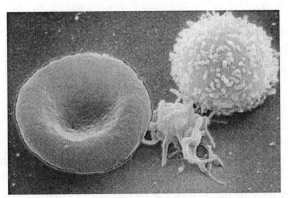

From Left to Right - Red Blood Cell, Platelet, White Blood Cell

Platelets

Platelets are cell fragments without nuclei that release blood-clotting chemicals at the site of wounds. They do this by adhering to the walls of blood vessels, thereby plugging the rupture in the vascular wall. There are more than a dozen types of blood clotting factors and platelets that need to interact in the blood clotting process. Recent research has shown that platelets help fight infections by releasing proteins that kill invading bacteria and other microorganisms and by stimulating the immune system. Individual platelets are about 1/3 the size of red cells and have a lifespan of 9-10 days. Like the red and white blood cells, platelets are produced in bone marrow from stem cells. A cubic millimeter of human blood contains about 200-300 thousand platelets.

Plasma

Plasma is the liquid portion of blood and makes up approximately 60% of our blood's volume. Plasma is comprised of 90% water and 10% blood clotting factors, sugars, lipids, vitamins, minerals, hormones, enzymes, antibodies, and other proteins. As the heart pumps blood to all of the cells throughout the body, the plasma carries nourishment to each cell and serves as the media that carries away the waste products of the cells metabolism.

Antibodies

Antibodies are elements in the plasma whose job it is to identify foreign red blood cells that have entered the blood. If foreign red blood cells are found, the antibodies "glue" the foreign red blood cells together causing them to agglutinate or clump together. The body agglutinates these foreign red blood cells together because clumps of red blood cells are easier for the body to dispose of than individual foreign red blood cells. An agglutination test is always performed before a blood transfusion is given to a patient in order to make sure that the blood to be infused is compatible with the patient's.

Bloods Origin

A child's blood type is received from the father. An unborn child's blood is produced within the child itself. The mother does not contribute one drop of blood to her offspring.

An unfertilized ovum can never develop blood because the female egg does not, by itself, contain the elements essential for the production of blood. It is only after the male element has entered the ovum that blood develops. Studying a common chicken egg can easily validate this. In an unfertilized egg, no blood ever appears and no baby chick develops. However, blood appears just a few hours after the male element has added life to the egg and a chick embryo develops. Hence the truth of Scripture; **"... the life of the flesh *is* in the blood:"** (Lev 17:11). And because there is no life in the egg until the male element unites with it, it is easily concluded that the male element is the source of the blood, or said another way, the male element is the source of the life of the body.

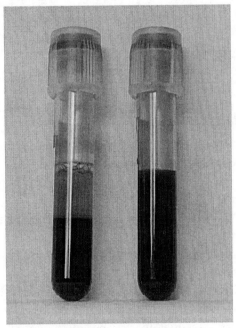

Agglutinated Blood   Whole Blood

The mother provides the fetus with the nutritive elements for the building of the body, but all of the embryo's blood, is formed in the embryo itself. From the time of conception to the time of birth not one single drop of blood ever passes from mother to child. The placenta is constructed so that all the necessary soluble nutritive elements such as proteins, fats, carbohydrates, salts, minerals and even antibodies pass freely from mother to child and the waste products of the child's metabolism are passed back to the mother's circulatory system, no actual interchange of a single drop of blood ever occurs.

Sinful Blood

Human blood is a corrupting agent because the red blood cells contain sin. Shortly after death, decay sets in, and it first begins in the blood. This is why Undertakers replace a cadaver's blood with embalming fluid and meat will spoil unless it is completely drained of blood.

The corrupting nature of sinful blood was dramatically demonstrated by the first miracle God performed in response to Pharaoh's hard heartedness; **"And the LORD said unto Moses, Pharaoh's heart is hardened, he refuseth to let the people go. Get thee unto Pharaoh in the morning; lo, he goeth out unto the water; and thou shalt stand by the river's brink against he come; and the rod which was turned to a serpent shalt thou take in thine hand. And thou shalt say unto him, The LORD God of the Hebrews hath sent me unto thee, saying, Let my people go, that they may serve me in the wilderness: and, behold, hitherto thou wouldest not hear. Thus saith the LORD, In this thou shalt know that I am the LORD:**

behold, I will smite with the rod that is in mine hand
upon the waters which are in the river, and they shall
be turned to blood. And the fish that is in the river
shall die, and the river shall stink; and the Egyptians
shall loathe to drink of the water of the river. And
the LORD spake unto Moses, Say unto Aaron, Take
thy rod, and stretch out thine hand upon the waters
of Egypt, upon their streams, upon their rivers, and
upon their ponds, and upon all their pools of water,
that they may become blood; and that there may
be blood throughout all the land of Egypt, both in
vessels of wood, and in vessels of stone. And Moses
and Aaron did so, as the LORD commanded; and he
lifted up the rod, and smote the waters that were in
the river, in the sight of Pharaoh, and in the sight of
his servants; and all the waters that were in the river
were turned to blood. And the fish that was in the
river died; and the river stank, and the Egyptians
could not drink of the water of the river; and there
was blood throughout all the land of Egypt. And the
magicians of Egypt did so with their enchantments:
and Pharaoh's heart was hardened, neither did he
hearken unto them; as the LORD had said. And
Pharaoh turned and went into his house, neither did
he set his heart to this also. And all the Egyptians
digged round about the river for water to drink; for
they could not drink of the water of the river. And
seven days were fulfilled, after that the LORD had
smitten the river" (Ex 7:14-25).

This plague graphically illustrates several facts
regarding man's corrupt blood:

- It disproves the alleged supremacy of nature. No

matter what man may think, God is in control.

- It shows that sinful blood by itself only corrupts and defiles and has no intrinsic value in itself.
- It points out, by way of Pharaoh's magicians, that sinful man is fully capable of corrupting whatever he touches because the magicians did not have the slightest trouble corrupting pure water into what was unfit for human consumption.
- It instructs us, by way of the toxic effect the corrupted water had upon the fish, the corruptive nature of blood is irreversible and lethal.
- It illustrates, by way of the people digging for water, man's need, desire and thirst for pure, living water. Jesus Christ said; **"… whosoever drinketh of the water that I shall give him shall never thirst; but the water that I shall give him shall be in him a well of water springing up into everlasting life"** (Jn 4:14).

Man's blood is corrupt but Christ's blood is pure and uncorrupted by sin. David said Jesus' body should not see corruption. This prophecy was fulfilled to the letter. After Jesus' death on the cross, Joseph of Arimathaea **"wrapped it [Jesus' body] in a clean linen cloth, And laid it in his own new tomb, which he had hewn out in the rock: and he rolled a great stone to the door of the sepulcher, and departed."** (Matt 27:59-60). Jesus did not say dead, nor did his body start to corrupt as a mortal's would have, **"… he rose again the third day according to the scriptures:"** (1 Cor 15:4 because His blood was sinless. The Bible further confirms this fact, Jesus Himself informing us; **"… I lay down my life,** that I might take it again. No man taketh it from me, but I lay it down of myself. I have power to lay it down, and I have power to take it again. ..."(Jn 10:17-18). He arose by His own power because He was sinless and consequently, death had no claim on Him because **"In him was life;"** (Jn 1:4). **"For as the Father [God] hath life in himself; so hath he [God] given to the Son [Jesus] to have life in himself;"** (Jn 5:26).

<u>Blood Exists Forever</u>

Blood exists forever. This fact has been scientifically proven by the extraction of blood proteins from ancient ground samples. The important thing to note however is that the unjustly shed blood of the redeemed continually calls out to God for justice; **"And Abel, he also brought of the firstlings of his flock and of the fat thereof. And the LORD had respect unto Abel and to his offering: But unto Cain and to his offering he had not respect. And Cain was very wroth, and his countenance fell. And Cain talked with Abel his brother: and it came to pass, when they were in the field, that Cain rose up against Abel his brother, and slew him. And the LORD said unto Cain, Where is Abel thy brother? And he said, I know not: Am I my brother's keeper? And he said, What hast thou done? The voice of thy brother crieth unto me from the ground."** (Gen 4:5-10).

And so it is with all the blood of the saints that the life that is in the blood is forever crying out to God for revenge; **"... they [the saints] cried with a loud voice, saying, How long, O Lord, holy and true, dost thou not judge and avenge our blood on them that**

dwell on the earth?" (Rev 6:10).   Note this and note it well, God will avenge in the fullness of time; **"...for it is written "Vengeance is mine; I will repay, saith the Lord."** (Rom 12:19), **"And I will execute great vengeance upon them with furious rebukes; and they shall know that I am the LORD, when I shall lay my vengeance upon them."** (Ez 25:17).

Recently, an interesting case supporting the Biblical fact that blood exists forever has come to light. In 1990 a Tyrannosaurus Rex skeleton (a pre-flood dinosaur) was unearthed in the United States. When the bones were brought to the Montana State University's lab, it was noticed some parts deep inside the long bone of the leg had not completely fossilized and that the bone contained blood vessel channels complete with blood protein hemoglobin.   5,000+ year old blood was still intact.

Blood Is Wealth

"His substance also was seven thousand sheep, and three thousand camels, and five hundred yoke of oxen, and five hundred she asses, and a very great household; so that this man was the greatest of all the men of the east." (Job 1:3). In Old Testament days, and so in a lesser degree today, a person's wealth is in part calculated based upon the amount of his possessions. In an agrarian society wealth is calculated by the number and bloodline of their livestock. This is so because livestock provided transportation, food, and clothing and determines the extent of hospitality the owner could extend to others. One with a large herd could spare an animal for a special meal to entertain guests. One with a meager herd could not risk decreasing the herd below the critical point for herd reproduction. A person's social status was inseparable from the number of domesticated animals he possessed.

Every husbandman knows that the bloodline of his livestock is of great importance. This is why high stud fees are charged for registered thoroughbred horses and cattle. Consequently, the animals presented to the High Priests for temple sacrifices brought home the true significance of faith to a degree that most do not appreciate today. It took a great deal of faith for a person who's livelihood depended upon the number, health and physical attributes of his livestock to sacrifice his best, healthiest and most perfect animal, knowing that this beast would have been his breeding stock of choice. To give it to the Lord for a sacrifice was visible proof that he believed that the Lord was truly able to provide all his needs from the remaining inferior livestock.

God's Law

Genesis Chapter 1 informs us that God created the heavens and the earth. With this creation God also established laws for its operation. These laws are commonly, but incorrectly, known as the Laws of Nature or Natural Laws. These in fact should rightly be called God's Laws governing His creation because He established them and like God himself, they change not.

After creating Adam and Eve, God placed these first two humans in the Garden of Eden to dress and keep it. In addition to these assigned duties, God also gave Adam and Eve the first ever civil code to govern their behavior; **"The LORD God took the man, and**

**put him into the Garden of Eden to dress it and keep
it. And the LORD God commanded the man saying,
Of every tree of the garden thou mayest freely eat:
But of the tree of the knowledge of good and evil,
thou shalt not eat of it: for in the day that thou eatest
thereof thou shalt surely die."** (Gen 2:15-17).

Now because God made Adam and Eve free moral
agents He also had to make them subject to law. The
concept of law is very important and the full significance
thereof is vital to the understanding and appreciation of
the salvation that is freely offered to us through Jesus
Christ.

Noah Webster's 1828 dictionary defines law as
"*A rule, particularly an established or permanent
rule, prescribed by the supreme power of a state to its
subjects, for regulating their actions, particularly their
social actions.*" Said another way, *law* denotes the rule
of action that God has laid down or assigned for the
government of man in his relations to his creator and his
fellow-creatures.

There are only three types of civil law and all three
are found in Scripture:
1. Imperative or mandatory; commanding one what
   shall be done
2. Prohibitory; restraining one from what is to be
   forborne
3. Permissive; declaring what one may do without
   incurring a penalty

There are three main points regarding this civil law,
or rule of action for man, that should be fully understood:

First, God's civil code (rule of action for man) is
right and proper for man to observe. **"The law is holy,**

and commandment holy, and just, and good." (Rom 7:12). It is the expression of the will of a righteous God concerning the way He would have us feel and act, and hence its requirements cannot be wrong. No one can rightfully say that there is anything unjust or unbecoming in commanding us to love the Lord our God with all the heart, and with all the soul, and with all the strength, and with all our mind, and our neighbors as ourselves. Even a cursory review of world history will affirm that observing God's law is beneficial to man and raises man's standard of living and social morals. The proof of this fact is easily verified when one compares and contrasts the affect Christianity has had on European culture with any other culture. One will note a marked difference in personal morals, value of human life, generosity, care for one's fellow man, and industrial accomplishments.

    __Second__, God's civil code applies to all aspects of our life. It applies to our thoughts, emotions, and desires as well as words and deeds. God's law demands supreme, unfaltering, unceasing love toward God and to our fellow men; **"Jesus said unto him, Thou shalt love the Lord thy God with all thy heart, and with all thy soul, and with all thy mind. This is the first and great commandment. And the second *is* like unto it, Thou shalt love thy neighbour as thyself. On these two commandments hang all the law and the prophets."** (Matt 22:37-40). Hence it is written, **"Love is the fulfilling of the law."** (Rom 13:10).

    Due to the demanding requirements of the law, no man can completely comply with it. Outwardly, one may appear to conform to the highest standards of human integrity, but **"the Lord seeth not as man seeth; for man looketh on the outward appearance, but the Lord looketh on the heart"** (1 Sam 16:7) and **"The heart *is* deceitful above all *things*, and desperately wicked: who can know it? I the LORD search the heart, I try the reins, even to give every man according to his ways, *and* according to the fruit of his doings."** (Jer 17:9-10). Because man is sinful, full of sin (red blood cells containing sin interact with every single cell in a person's body), it is impossible for anyone to keep the law in its entirety. To an unregenerate sinner a lustful look is just that, a look, no action taken hence no sin, and no violation of the law. But to God, a lustful look is adultery (Matt 5:28) and the inner feelings of hate is murder (1 Jn 3:15).

Third, God's law consists of two parts: a command, and a penalty for disobedience. Without a penalty, it could not be a law. Law cannot exist unless it carries with it rewards and punishments to encourage and enforce obedience. Human governments never impose a law for their citizens without an appropriate penalty attached to it. The simple reason is that it could not, and would not be a law at all if it were not empowered with a punishment for the transgression or neglect of its requirements.

In God's divine government, just like our own worldly governments, a penalty is connected with every rule of action that has been laid down for our guidance. If the law is violated, penalty is inevitable. Sometimes it is executed instantly, but more often than not, it is long delayed, never the less, sooner or later justice is served. It is this delay that man mistakes for tolerance and so evil persists and reigns supreme in this present world; "**... because sentence against an evil work is not executed speedily, therefore the heart of the sons of men is fully set in them to do evil.**" (Ecc. 8:11). Hopefully one realizes that the reason divine justice is not instantly meted out when sin is committed is due solely to God's "**... longsuffering to us-ward, not willing that any should perish, but that all should come to repentance.**" (2 Pet 3:9).

Sin

Adam and Eve violated God's civil code (rule of action) and ate of the tree of knowledge of good and evil that was in the midst of the Garden of Eden. When Adam willfully partook of the forbidden fruit, "**... Adam was not deceived...**" (1 Tim 2:14). We are told, "**... the eyes of them both were opened, and they knew that they were naked, and they sewed fig-leaves together, and made themselves aprons**" (Gen 3.7). Upon violation, the law invoked its penalty for the violation; "**... thou shalt surely die [the curse].**" (Gen 2.17). And sure enough, everyone will die, some sooner than others, but all will die eventually, so remember; "**... dust thou art, and unto dust shalt thou return**" (Gen 3:19). Every single person on earth knows that death awaits them; "**As it is appointed unto men once to die, but after this the judgment:**" (Heb 9:27).

Adam's partaking of the forbidden fruit was man's first violation of the law and the consequence for this violation is referred to as "sin" in the Bible. 1 John 3:4 makes the definition of this term sin very clear; "**... sin is the transgression of the law.**" Or said in another way, sin is the violation of God's civil code, whether it is in thought, emotion, desire, word or deed.

Initially, Adam and Eve were sinless for they communed with the LORD in the garden in cool of the day. They were "**... clothed with robes of righteousness ...**" (Isa. 61:10) and being pure and so clothed, "**... all things are pure ...**" (Titus 1:15) hence they were not ashamed that they were physically naked as stated in Genesis 2:25; they "**...were both naked, the man and his wife, and were not ashamed.**"

Their persona also had a divine glow about them like Moses' face shown after being the presence of the LORD: "**... the children of Israel saw the face of Moses, that the skin of Moses' face shone: and Moses put the veil upon his face again ...**" (Ex 34:35). Being sinless, the light that God puts in every person's heart shone through the flesh undiminished by sin; "**... the life was the light of men.**" (Jn 1:4) and "***That* was the true Light, which lighteth every man that cometh into the world.**" (Jn 1:9).

In their original and sinless state, Adam and Eve were created with spiritual sight, and were unaffected or "blind" to the lusts of the flesh and the physical world. We know this because Satan told Eve; "**... Ye shall not surely die: For God doth know that in the day ye eat thereof, then your eyes shall be opened, and ye shall be as gods, knowing good and evil.**" (Gen 3:4-5). Adam and Eve did not know the lust of the eyes, the lust of the flesh, or the pride of life.

Unfortunately, with Satan's prompting and intimating that there was something more than one could and should experience, Eve was deceived into thinking God was withholding something good from her and the lusts of her flesh were awakened. Eve should have known **"… the LORD will give grace and glory: no good thing will he withhold from them that walk uprightly."** (Psm 84:11) but Satan's intimations were too strong and she partook of the forbidden fruit.

Instantly Eve's appearance became carnal, the divine glow ceased to illuminate her persona. Her new carnal appearance and new lustful nature obviously had a significant influence upon Adam. He succumbed to Eve's enticements only to realize too late that **"… the lips of a strange woman drop as an honeycomb, and her mouth is smoother than oil: But her end is bitter as wormwood, sharp as a two-edged sword. Her feet go down to death; her steps take hold on hell."** (Prov 5:3-5). Instead of turning to the Lord for assistance as Scripture directs us to do; **"For the LORD shall be thy confidence, and shall keep thy foot from being taken."** (Prov 3:26) and **"forget not my law; but let thine heart keep my commandments; For length of days, and long life, and peace, shall they add to thee."** (Prov 3:1), he succumbed to Eve's promptings, knowing that what he was doing was in direct contradiction to the LORD's commandment.

Adam knew full well, **"… if sinners entice thee, consent thou not."** (Prov 1:10). Nonetheless, he succumbed to Eve's promptings and willfully transgressed God's law the moment he decided to partake of the tree of the knowledge of good and evil. Adam succumbed **"… to the strange woman, even from the stranger which flattereth with her words; Which forsaketh the guide of her youth, and**

forgetteth the covenant of her God. For her house
inclineth unto death, and her paths unto the dead.
None that go unto her return again, neither take they
hold of the paths of life."** (Prov 2:16-19), he was not
bamboozled. This very same path is still trod today:
Satan tempts, man voluntarily transgresses and God
inflicts the penalty for the violation. Therefore, **"...
incline thine ear unto wisdom, and apply thine heart
to understanding"**! (Prov 2:2).

It was at this point that sin entered into the world
and their eyes were opened to the lusts of the flesh and
the allures of the physical world as stated in Genesis
3:7; **"And the eyes of them both were opened, and
they knew that they were naked; and they sewed
fig leaves together, and made themselves aprons"**
for **"...unto them that are defiled and unbelieving *is*
nothing pure; but even their minds and consciences
is defiled."** (Tit. 1:15). And so it has ever been with
mankind; **"... because ye have sinned against the
LORD, and have not obeyed the voice of the LORD,
nor walked in his law, nor in his statutes, nor in his
testimonies; therefore this evil is happened unto you
..."** (Jer 44:23).

Adam **"... plowed wickedness, [he] reaped
iniquity, [he ate] the fruit of lies; because [he] didst
trusted in [his own] way ..."** (Hos 10-13). He violated
God's law of sowing and reaping: **"Sow to yourselves
in righteousness, reap in mercy ..."** (Hosea 10:12)
for **"They that observe lying vanities forsake their
own mercy."** (Jonah 2:8). What a sad day for mankind,
but Praise God, **"... that through his name [Jesus]
whosoever believeth in him shall receive remission**

of sins." (Acts 10:42-43).

One of the things Satan failed to mention to Adam and Eve was one of the consequences for willful transgression of God's law. He failed to mention that once they knew sin they could never be sinless again. Because Adam was in the transgression by willfully sinning and Eve "...was the mother of all living ..." (Gen 3:20) we are all sinners because surely we are the flesh and bone of Adam and Eve.

It is because our blood type is inherited from our father, which traces all the way back to Adam, that "... they [all men] proceed from evil to evil, and they know not me, saith the Lord" (Jer 9:3). Therefore "... there is no man that sinneth not,"(I Kings 8:46). Ecclesiastes 7:20 states "... there is not a just man upon earth, that doeth good, and sinneth not ...", consequently all men are cursed. "Thus saith the Lord; Cursed be the man that trusteth in man, and maketh flesh his arm, and whose heart departeth from the LORD." (Jer 17:5). "...Cursed is every one that continueth not in all things which are written in the book of the law to do them." (Gal 3:10), "... the scripture hath concluded all under sin ..." (Gal 3:22) and "... the wages of sin is death ..." (Rom 6:23). Neither you nor I are an exception because there are no exceptions.

Sinless Blood

Adam's sin placed man in a precarious position. According to God's law the only way to atone for Adam's sin was through the shedding of blood. The law is very clear on this point, "... without shedding of

blood is no remission [of sin]…" (Heb 9:22). Therefore because man sinned, man's blood was required to be shed in payment.

The problem for man was, the man whose blood must be shed in payment for sin must be innocent and without sin, (i.e. without spot or blemish). But as we saw above, there is none righteous, no not one. Therefore the question before man was, who could possibly serve as a suitable sacrifice? Fortunately God provided the answer and the solution. God would, in the fullness of time provide the suitable sacrifice for mans sin. He would provide it via the seed of the woman, and the Saviour would provide remission for the sin of the world and bruise Satan's head for his wicked deed.

Man was directed to look forward to the coming of the promised Saviour. Animal sacrifices were to be made until such time to keep man in remembrance of what sinners we are, how hopeless our condition is without a Saviour, how disdainful willful flesh is to God, and how the shedding of the Saviour's blood would redeem us. The first-born Son of God, Jesus Christ, is that Saviour. In the fullness of time God provided His only begotten Son to be the propitiation for our sins. Jesus Christ came, sacrificed Himself on our behalf and washed our sins away in His own blood. Why? Because **"… God is love."** (1 Jn 4:8) and **"… the love of Christ, … passeth knowledge, [our ability to understand] …"** (Eph 3:19). In fact, **"God commendeth his love toward us, in that, while we were sinners, Christ died for us."** (Rom 5:8). Nobody can fully comprehend it, nobody can fully explain it. All one can do is to humbly accept what God has freely done for us. We can and should accept God's free gift of salvation provided through Jesus Christ our Saviour because **"Neither is there salvation in any other: for there is none other name under heaven given among men, whereby we must be saved."** (Acts 4:12) from the damnation of Hell.

Satan

The power of Satan's deception lies in the fact that he is the consummate liar. Satan knows just the right lie to stir-up our lustful appetite. This is why God tells us **"The simple believeth every word; but the prudent man looketh well to his going."** (Prov 14:15) and that you must **"... therefore be wise as serpents, and harmless as doves."** (Matt 10:16).

Yes, Satan is not only a liar but the originator of the act of lying and only tells half-truths at best. The Bible tells us; **"...[Satan] was a murderer from the beginning, and abode not in the truth, because there is no truth in him. When he speaketh a lie, he speaketh of his own: for he is a liar, and the father of it."** (Jn 8:44). Christ came to **"... open [our] eyes, and to turn [us] from darkness to light, and *from* the power of Satan unto God, that [we] may receive forgiveness of sins, and inheritance among them which are sanctified by faith that is in [Christ]"** (Acts 26:18) because we are blind spiritually and only have eyes for the physical. This is why the Apostle Paul commands us to **"...walk by faith not by sight...."** (2 Cor 5:7).

One should not delude one's self, there definitely exists a spiritual realm. It may be currently unseen and uncared about by most of humanity but it exists in all its grandeur nonetheless. Adam and Eve could see the heavenly host, John the Baptist **"...saw the heavens opened..."** (Mk 1:10), Elisha prayed, and said **"... LORD, I pray thee, open his eyes, that he may see, And the LORD opened the eyes of the young man; and he saw: and, behold, the mountain was full of horses and chariots of fire round about Elisha."** (2 Kings 6:17).

Our eyes have been opened just as Satan said they would be, but he failed to mention that the lusts of the flesh (the physical body wherein our soul resides) would be stirred into action. Once the soul turned from the spiritual to the carnal **"... the eye is not satisfied with seeing, nor the ear filled with hearing."** (Ecc 1:8). It is the insatiable lust of the eyes, the insatiable lust of the flesh and the pride of life that drives men to stumble down the dark pathways of sin. It is the vain attempt to satiate fleshly lusts that cause man to continually seek pleasure in the physical realm instead of the spiritual.

God's law was for our own protection but man willfully violated it. The world became hostile and wicked **"...because ye have sinned against the LORD, and have not obeyed the voice of the LORD, nor walked in his law, nor in his statutes, nor in his testimonies; therefore this evil is happened unto you ..."** (Jer 44:23). It is for this reason the world waxes worse and worse. It is for this reason sin reigns in our world today. The Biblical truth that every man, woman and child should take note of is; **"There is a way which seemeth right unto man, but the end thereof are the ways of death."** (Prov 14:12) because **"heart is deceitful above all things, and desperately** wicked..." (Jer 17:9).

Satan never speaks of sin's consequences, and they are rarely thought about, yet they will go far beyond what one could ever expect. Case in point;

- Satan is absolutely correct in saying you can be "cool" if you smoke. However what Satan fails to mention is that you will only be "cool" until you become incontinent. (Incontinence is a much more common consequence of smoking than lung cancer).
- Satan is absolutely correct in saying that you can experience euphoria if you take various and sundry drugs. However what Satan fails to mention is that you will only experience euphoria until every synapse in your brain is fried, and you are reduced to permanent state of semi-consciousness.
- Satan is absolutely correct in saying you can live wild and free. However what Satan fails to mention is that you will only be wild and free until your loins are rotted out by venereal disease.

One should always remember that Satan is extremely powerful and is capable of giving us the world. He offered it to Christ; "... **the devil taketh him up into an exceeding high mountain, and sheweth him all the kingdoms of the world, and the glory of them; And saith unto him, All these things will I give thee, if thou wilt fall down and worship me."** (Matt 4:8-9). Note the great omission very carefully. Satan says you can have it all but what he does not tell you is that you can only have what he gives you for a short time. The more Satan gives you, the shorter the time you can possess it. The antichrist will experience this truth in the end times. In return for his worship of Satan, all his fleshly desires will be fulfilled to the uttermost. The lust of his eyes, the lust of his flesh and his pride of life will be fully indulged and pandered to with all Satan can provide. However, he will not be able to retain all his worldly pleasures for more than seven years, because the wages of sin **is** death, and "**... the Lord shall consume with the spirit of his mouth, and shall destroy with the brightness of his coming:**" "**... I [the Lord] will punish the world for their evil, and the wicked for *their* iniquity; and I will cause the arrogancy of the proud to cease, and will lay low the haughtiness of the terrible.**" (Isa 13:11). Judgement is coming, there are no *ifs, ands* or *buts* about it.

Leprosy

The Bible informs us that all have sinned and there is none righteous, no not one, because men "**... proceed from evil to evil ...**" (Jer 9:3) and God visits "**...the iniquity of the fathers upon the children unto the third and fourth generation of them that hate me,**" (Deut 5:9). Also it is clear from our own daily experiences and observations that sin is progressive in nature. It is a common occurrence to see wicked men growing worse and worse under the influence of their own personal sin. Timothy 3:13 confirms this observation by saying "**... evil men and seducers shall wax worse and worse ...**" It is also clear that initially, men are never initially as bad as sin can make them. If they were, there would be no downward spiral of human depravity. This progressive nature of sin is why leprosy is used in the Bible as a symbolic of sin.

There have always been diseases that were more painful, more contagious, and equally afflictive as leprosy, however leprosy is singled out from all other diseases of the world because it pictures the progressive and debilitating nature of sin. Leprosy provides the perfect picture of how the worst and most abominable transgressions can grow out of the smallest of beginnings.

Leprosy begins within the body and is often in the system three to twelve years before it manifests itself. The first visible signs of leprosy, like sin, are often very minute, and not easily detected. It is from these smallest of beginnings that the living death of the leper develops. It is only by degree and through the course of years, that it transforms its victim into a living embodiment of death. It is by degree that leprosy consumes the body from the inside out. The characteristic loss of fingers and toes is not due to the phalanges falling off but rather absorption by the body itself. The body actually gradually self-consumes itself illustrating that sin is a personal and consuming condition not an affliction from without. All it may take is a look, hearing a suggestion, or receiving an inappropriate touch and Satan has gained a foothold. And like leprosy, no man can tell what the smallest sin left unchecked, may progress into.

Mans progressive sinfulness is also highlighted throughout the Holy Scriptures; **"And God looked upon the earth, and, behold, it was corrupt; for all flesh had corrupted his way upon the earth."**(Gen 6:12). **"Because that, when they knew God, they glorified** *him* **not as God, neither were thankful; but became vain in their imaginations, and their** foolish heart was darkened. Professing themselves to be wise, they became fools, And changed the glory of the incorruptible God into an image made like to corruptible man, and to birds, and four-footed beasts, and creeping things. Wherefore God also gave them up to uncleanness through the lusts of their own hearts, to dishonour their own bodies between themselves; Who changed the truth of God into a lie, and worshipped and served the creature more than the Creator, who is blessed for ever. Amen. For this cause God gave them up unto vile affections: for even their women did change the natural use into that which is against nature: And likewise also the men, leaving the natural use of the woman, burned in their lust one toward another; men with men working that which is unseemly, and receiving in themselves that recompense of their error which was meet. And even as they did not like to retain God in *their* knowledge, God gave them over to a reprobate mind, to do those things which are not convenient; Being filled with all unrighteousness, fornication, wickedness, covetousness, maliciousness; full of envy, murder, debate, deceit, malignity; whisperers, Backbiter, haters of God, despiteful, proud, boasters, inventors of evil things, disobedient to parents, Without understanding, covenant-breakers, without natural affection, implacable, unmerciful: Who knowing the judgment of God, that they which commit such things are worthy of death, not only do the same, but have pleasure in them that do them." (Rom 1:21-32). Without a doubt, "… evil men and seducers shall wax worse and worse …" (2 Tim 3:13).

A leper is a walking dead man, and so likewise is sinful man. However without spiritual sight we are deluded into thinking all is well. In reality, man is degraded, corrupt and wallows in the filthiness of his own fleshly lusts. In a word he is unholy. Isaiah describes the state of sinful man this way; **"From the sole of the foot even unto the head, *there* is no soundness in it; *but* wounds, and bruises, and putrefying sores, they have not been closed, neither bound up, neither mollified with ointment."** But in spite of our sinful nature **"… God commendeth his love toward us, in that, while we were yet sinners, Christ died for us."** (Rom 5:8). It is by the grace of God, and only by the grace of God, that the Lord provided a means of cleansing us from sin. It is the blood of Christ that will **"Wash [you] thoroughly from [your] iniquity, and cleanses [you] from [your] sin."** (Psm 51:2).

As stated earlier, sin like leprosy is progressive. No man ever starts out with deliberate resolve, much less the remotest idea of becoming a drunkard. But small beginnings, harmless in themselves, whet an appetite, which becomes a habit, which grows into an insatiable addiction, which grows into an all-consuming obsession, transforming man into a bleary-eyed, foul-mouthed, disgusting wretch, who destroys his own life, dishonors his family name and disgraces his community. Never, never forget that any sin, no matter how small it may seem, has the potential to grow into a greater sin.

The progressive nature of sin also used to be referred to as a vice in the old days. In fact every large metropolitan city had a vice squad as part of their police force. And like leprosy, a vice (today it is spelled *vise*) is a perfect picture of sin's effect on a person. Once a vice has its grip upon your soul you are truly caught in the jaws of a vise, escape becomes impossible. Your vice becomes a self-consuming obsession as Satan ever so slowly screws the jaws of the vise closed. Each revolution the jackscrew crushes the soul just a little bit more, making salvation all the more unlikely and unobtainable. Mercy is never proffered and there is no way to escape without a Saviour. And so it is by these small, innocuous steps a man becomes a drunkard or a dope addict. Do not be deceived, any sin may lead a man into the depths of depravity. The lust of the flesh knows no bounds. Sin knows no limits. He that hath an ear, let him hear.

Punishment

Death is the prescribed punishment for transgression of the law, whether it is in thought, emotion, desire, word or deed. Romans 6:23 informs us **"...the wages of sin is death..."** Wages is defined in Webster's 1828 dictionary *as "recompense or that which is received in return"*. Expressed in another way, the price you will have to pay for being a sinner is death. That is as plain and simple as it can get. And this is exactly what Romans 5:17-18 says; **"... by one man's [Adam] offence death reigned by one [Adam]"** and **"by the offence of one [Adam] judgment came upon all men to condemnation ..."**

The sad truth is that while the word death may not seem so terrible in our "modern and enlightened" society whose primary occupation is the detached, vicarious experiencing of death via Hollywood's movies and such like, the truth is, death is an extremely serious matter.

Admittedly, some people dismiss the concept that death is an eternal state of suffering for the soul. Rutherford, one of the leaders of Jehovah's Witnesses, taught that death is a period of absolute non-existence. The dead are entirely unconscious in the grave and do not suffer because they do not exist. The Seventh Day Adventists teach that death is a state of silence, inactivity, and unconsciousness. Such statements should come as no surprise for theories of this ilk have abounded for centuries. All such theories concerning reincarnation, soul sleep, unconsciousness, eternal inactivity, etc. are nothing more than vain flights of fancy and unsubstantiated hopes that man will not have to stand before a thrice Holy God in judgement.

The Bible unequivocally refutes all the vain notions of man; **"...there are many devices in a man's heart; nevertheless the counsel of the Lord, that shall stand."** (Prov 19:21). Hence the old but very true saying- *Man proposes but God disposes!* And the counsel of the Lord is; **"... it is appointed unto men once to die, but after this the judgement."** (Heb 9:27). So, man can disregard the scriptural truth and continue to propose as many theories regarding death as their imaginations can concoct however, none of them change the fact that everyone's physical body will die, and death will be a permanent and eternal state of suffering for the unbelieving soul.

Those that reject Jesus Christ as their Lord and Saviour experience not just one death but two. They that are born only once, (do not experience the new birth provided by salvation) will die twice. The first death the unbeliever experiences is that of the physical body. At this juncture the body and soul are separated. The physical body goes to the grave and the soul is damned to Hell. Do not let anyone deceive you, Hell is real! Every earthquake serves as a grim reminder that Hell is ever expanding beneath our feet due to the continual influx of damned souls and every volcanic eruption is a terrifying testimony that the flames of Hell burn just as hot today as they did in centuries past.

Bible truth cannot be circumvented, philosophically dismissed or intellectualized away: if you die without ever receiving Jesus Christ as your Saviour, your body will go to the grave and your soul will be damned to Hell. Voltaire, the famous atheist, found this truth out the hard way. It is reported that while on his deathbed, lying in a state of semi-consciousness, Voltaire suddenly sat bolt upright, and wide-eyed screamed out, *"The dogs of Hell have come for my soul!"* After this outburst, he fell back into bed, dead!

Hell is a dark pit where your soul hangs suspended against the side thereof in torment from flames, **"Where their worm dieth not, and the fire is not quenched."** (Mk 9:44). It is the last place you should ever want to go.

The physician Luke gives a graphic description of a person's first moments in Hell; **"There was a certain rich man, which was clothed in purple and fine linen, and fared sumptuously every day: And there was a certain beggar named Lazarus, which was laid at his gate full of sores, And desiring to be fed with the crumbs which fell from the rich man's table: moreover the dogs came and licked his sores. And it**

came to pass, that the beggar died, and was carried by the angels into Abraham's bosom: the rich man also died, and was buried; And in hell he lift up his eyes, being in torments, and seeth Abraham afar off, and Lazarus in his bosom. And he cried and said, Father Abraham, have mercy on me, and send Lazarus, that he may dip the tip of his finger in water, and cool my tongue: for I am tormented in this flame. But Abraham said, Son, remember that thou in thy lifetime receivest thy good things, and likewise Lazarus evil things: but now he is comforted, and thou art tormented. And beside all this, between us and you there is a great gulf fixed: so that they which would pass from hence to you cannot: neither can they pass to us, that would come from thence." (Lk 16:19-31).

However, as bad as Hell is, it is just the "holding cell" for the unbeliever's soul, (those that do not accept Christ as their Saviour). The damned soul will reside in Hell until the Great White Throne Judgement. At this appointed time all the souls in Hell will be resurrected back into the bodies they had while alive. One by one, each will be brought before the presiding judge, the Lord Jesus Christ . Each will bow the knee and confess that Jesus Christ is indeed Lord. Each will be judged for sins committed and then sentenced to the second and eternal death in the Lake of Fire.

Angels will execute the sentence by casting each and every damned soul that was resurrected from the flames of Hell, body and soul, headlong into the Lake of Fire. This is the second death spoken of in the Revelation of Jesus Christ to Saint John; **"... I saw a great white** throne, and him that sat on it, from whose face the earth and the heaven fled away; and there was found no place for them. And I saw the dead, small and great, stand before God; and the books were opened: and another book was opened, which is the book of life: and the dead were judged out of those things which were written in the books, according to their works. And the sea gave up the dead which were in it; and death and hell delivered up the dead which were in them: and they were judged every man according to their works." (Rev 11-13).

Once in the Lake of Fire the unbeliever will sink out of sight beneath the flaming surface because sin has weight as attested to by the Apostle Paul in Hebrews 12:1, "... let us lay aside every weight, and the sin which doth so easily beset us ..." and Psalms 56:22 tells us to "Cast thy burden upon the LORD". Job in Job 31:6 requests to "... be weighed in an even balance, that God may know mine integrity ..." and King Belshazzar was "... weighed in the balances ..." (Dan. 5:27), and found wanting. This fact that sin has weight is the origin behind the common expressions *chains of sin* and *the burden of sin*.

Salvation requires **"godly sorrow [which] worketh repentance to salvation ..."** (2 Cor 7:10) and it is the Holy Ghost *pricking* the heart that causes Godly sorrow. We know this pricking by the Holy Ghost is how the Apostle Paul was prompted to realize his need of salvation for **"... the Lord said, I am Jesus whom thou persecutest: it is hard for thee to kick against the pricks. And he [Paul] trembling and astonished said, Lord what wilt thou have me to do? ..."** (Acts

9:5-6). After Jesus' resurrection the Apostle Peter told a crowd **"that God hath made that same Jesus, whom ye have crucified, both Lord and Christ. Now when they heard *this*, they were pricked in their heart, and said unto Peter … what shall we do? Then Peter said unto them, Repent, and be baptized every one of you in the name of Jesus Christ for the remission of sins, and ye shall receive the gift of the Holy Ghost."** (Acts 2:36-38).

One must realize however, that the Holy Ghost can only prick a person's heart, thereby causing a person to repent, if He has access to the heart. It is speculated that sinning creates a crust that veils the heart, because Obadiah 10 states that **"…shame shall cover thee, and thou shalt be cut off for ever."**

Sin unabated creates a crust that eventually veils the whole heart. Moreover, a heart completely crusted over with sin, (without any voids, or holes), makes it impossible for the Holy Ghost to prick the heart and thereby cause Godly sorrow. This phenomenon is most commonly referred to as, a hardened heart.

Once the heart is completely crusted over with sin, salvation becomes impossible. At this point, you have lost the ability to retain the knowledge of God; **"And even as they did not like to retain God in their knowledge, God gave them over to a reprobate mind, to do those things which are not convenient."** (Rom 1:28). From this point on, the only thing that stands between you and eternal damnation is time. And, **"boast not thyself of tomorrow; for thou knowest not what a day may bring forth."** (Pr 27:1). Your fate is sealed, you doom is unalterable and inevitable, even if you beseech God with tears; **"Lest there *be* any fornicator, or profane person, as Esau, who for one morsel of meat sold his birthright. For ye know how that afterward, when he would have inherited the blessing, he was rejected: for he found no place of repentance, though he sought it carefully with tears."** (Heb 12:16-17).

Furthermore, the sin crust continually grows thicker and thicker with each indulgence of sin and the thicker it gets, the heavier and more impervious it becomes. Once your sin becomes an all-consuming obsession, it will consume you; **"Being filled with all unrighteousness, fornication, wickedness, covetousness, maliciousness; full of envy , murder, debate, deceit, malignity; whisperers, Backbiters, haters of God, despiteful, proud, boasters, inventors of evil things, disobedient to parents, Without understanding, covenant-breakers, without natural affection, implacable, unmerciful: Who knowing the judgment of God, that they which commit such things are worthy of death, not only do the same, but have pleasure in them that do them."** (Rom 1:29-32) and eternal damnation is inevitable.

Only the blood of Jesus can wash this crust of sin away. Salvation must be sought before the sin crust totally veils the heart. Salvation must be sought while the Holy Ghost can still prick the heart and thereby cause Godly sorrow, a.k.a. repentance; **"...godly sorrow worketh repentance to salvation not to be repented of: ..."** (2 Cor 7:10). This is why it is so important to be washed in the blood of Jesus at the earliest possible age.

Eliminating any condition or practice in one's life that would hinder the Holy Spirit's work of convicting a person of their need of salvation is such a serious matter that *three times* Jesus advises; **"...if thy hand offend thee, cut it off: it is better for thee to enter into life maimed, than having two hands to go into hell , into the fire that never shall be quenched: Where their worm dieth not, and the fire is not quenched. And if thy foot offend thee, cut it off: it is better for thee to enter halt into life, than having two feet to be cast into hell, into the fire that never shall be quenched: Where their worm dieth not, and the fire is not quenched; And if thine eye offend thee, pluck it out: it is better for thee to enter into the kingdom of God with one eye, than having two eyes to be cast into hell fire: Where their worm dieth not, and the fire is not quenched."** (Mk 9:43-48).

For any who might think they can delay salvation until it is "convenient", there are two very important facts to be aware of;

1. The Bible does not inform us how fast a sin crust will form on a person's heart. So, for all you know, today may be the last day that the Holy Ghost can prick your heart.

2. Several activities common to man, that if continued therein, are guaranteed to create an thick, heavy and impervious crust of sin; **"...neither fornicators, nor idolaters, nor adulterers, nor effeminate, nor abusers of themselves with mankind, Nor thieves, nor covetous, nor drunkards, nor revilers, nor extortioners, shall inherit the kingdom of God."** (1 Cor 6:9-10).

Sin also has a highly offensive odor associated with it too. It stinketh in the nostrils of God. The prayers of the saints are also likened to the smell of smoke but contrariwise to sin's offensive odor, they have a very pleasant fragrance that God savors; **"... golden vials full of odors, which are the prayers of saints..."** (Rev 5:8). **"And the smoke of the incense, which came with the prayers of the saints, ascended up before God."** (Rev 8:4).

The smell of sin as it is burnt off the unbelievers' hearts in the Lake of Fire produces the horrendous smell of brimstone (e.g. burning sulphur). The smoke from which, ascends upward from the Lake of Fire forever and ever; **"Whosoever was not found written in the book of life was cast into the lake of fire burning with brimstone."** (Rev 20:15, 19:20) **"...where the smoke of their torment ascendeth up for ever and ever: and they have no rest day nor night."** (Rev 14:11) and there **"...shall be weeping and gnashing of teeth."** (Matt 8:12).

The weight of the sin crust veiling a person's heart at the time of death determines how deeply they shall descend below the flaming waves of the Lake of Fire. The heavier the sin crust, the deeper they will sink, and the greater the amount of torment experienced. Hence, a person like General Joseph Stalin will suffer far greater torments than the average "good person".

The disembodied soul shall forever suffer in the unquenchable flames of the Lake of Fire. The physical body will be burnt to ashes, leaving the soul without a body **"... for dust thou *art*, and unto dust shalt thou return."** (Gen 3:19).

The disembodied soul shall be forever tormented by the insatiable cravings that dominated its earthly life, because the soul **"… yielded [its] members [the flesh] servants to uncleanness and to iniquity unto iniquity; …"** (Rom 6:19). Consequently, the eternally damned soul shall forever crave the sensations and stimulations provided by **"… the lust of the eyes, the lust of the flesh, and the pride of life."** (1 Jn 2:16), yet never, ever be able to satisfy them.

And not only that, but because the self-righteous soul refused to listen to the LORD when He said **"… Seek ye me, and ye shall live:"** (Amos 5:4) it shall have absolutely no remembrance of God whatsoever because, **"… in death** *there is* **no remembrance of thee [God]:"** (Psm 6:5). And so, such is the fate of those vessels of wrath fitted to destruction.

Reward

The Bible also makes it very clear that eternal life in Glory is available to those who have had their sins washed away by the blood of Jesus Christ. In fact, it is important to note that Jesus came expressly to seek and to save those who are lost **"… not willing that any should perish, but that all should come to repentance."** (2 Pet 3:9). The reward for placing your faith in the fact that Jesus Christ shed His blood to wash your sins away according the Scriptures is immortality in what is commonly referred to as Heaven.

We are given a partial description of Heaven in the Bible and it is a glorious place; **"For it is written, Eye hath not seen, nor ear heard, neither have entered into the heart of man, the things which God hath prepared for them that love him."** (1 Cor 2:9).

Our eternal dwelling place will be the eternal great

city called the Holy or New Jerusalem. The Apostle John described it as having; **"...a wall great and high, and has twelve gates, ... And the wall of the city had twelve foundations, ... And the city lieth foursquare, and the length is as large as the breadth: and .. measured twelve thousand furlongs. The length and the breadth and the height of it are equal. ... And the building of the wall of it was of jasper: and the city was pure gold, like unto clear glass. And the foundations of the wall of the city were garnished with all manner of precious stones. The first foundation was jasper; the second, sapphire; the third, a chalcedony; the fourth, an emerald; The fifth, sardonyx; the sixth, sardius; the seventh, chrysolyte; the eighth, beryl; the ninth. a topaz; the tenth, a chrysoprasus; the eleventh, a jacinth; the twelfth, an amethyst. And the twelve gates were twelve pearls: every several gate was of one pearl: and the street of the city was pure gold, as it were transparent glass. And the city had no need of the sun, neither of the moon, to shine in it: for the glory of God did lighten it, and the Lamb is the light thereof."** (Rev 21:10-23).

Now, who in their right mind would not want to live is such a glorious place in a perfect immortal body? However, the truth of the matter is, only those whose name is **"...written in the Lamb's Book of Life"** (Rev 21:27) will have that privilege. So you see, eternity stands before each and every one of us. Those that reject Jesus Christ as their Saviour will spend an eternity in the Lake of Fire that burneth with fire and brimstone but those that believe God, accept Jesus Christ as their Saviour, their name will be found written in the Lamb's book of life and shall spend eternity in the New Jerusalem.

Righteousness

And so it is an undisputed fact that **"... all have sinned and come short of the glory of God;"** (Rom 3:23). **"... There is none righteous, no, not one: There is none that understandeth, there is none that seeketh after God. They are all gone out of the way, they are together become unprofitable; there is none that doeth good, no, not one. Their throat *is* an open sepulcher; with their tongues they have used deceit; the poison of asps *is* under their lips: whose mouth *is* full of cursing and bitterness: Their feet *are* swift to shed blood: Destruction and misery *are* in their ways: and the way of peace have they not known: There is no fear of God before their eyes."** (Rom 3:10-18).   However, God is **"... not willing that any should perish, but that all should come to repentance."**(2 Pet 3:9).   Because **"... *As* I live, saith the Lord God, I have no pleasure in the death of the wicked ..."** (Ez 33:11).

Please note and very carefully consider that despite God's personal feelings on the matter and His desire **"... that the wicked turn from his way and live..."** (Ez 33:11). His Holy Law demands that **"... except ye repent, ye shall all likewise perish"** (Lk 13:3) because **"the law of the LORD is perfect..."** (Psm 19:7).

For those who might object saying, *it is not fair* or *I would prefer some other way*, may I remind you what God says; **"God is greater than man. ... he giveth not account of any of his matters."** (Job 33:12-

13). God was not obligated in any way shape or form to provide a means of salvation. It is strictly by grace that God has made a means whereby we can save our soul from the damnation of Hell. So, to put it in plain English, whether you like it or not there is only one way to save your soul and that is God's way. Deciding to take advantage of it is the most important decision a person will ever make on this side of the grave.

The Bible clearly informs us that Jesus will impute His righteousness to us and only a righteous soul can fellowship with God. The question before us is how does one become righteous before a thrice Holy God, re-establish fellowship with God and attain eternal life? What does the Bible say is the proper way to have your sins paid for and obtain salvation from the wages of sin? Let us examine the four possible ways.

1. Self-Righteousness

The majority of people believe, *if I am a good person, God will consider me righteous.* The line of logic goes something like this; if I do my best in life and do not rob, steal, or murder anyone, God will weigh my good works against my bad in the scale of justice. My good works will outweigh my bad and I will consequently, be declared righteous. It is an easy and comforting belief, unfortunately, all it really is, is conjecture. Scripture does not substantiate this line of reasoning.

Genesis makes it clear that man is capable of being righteous and was righteous at one time. According to Genesis 1:27 **"... God created man in his own image, in the image of God created he him: male and female**

created he them". It follows directly that because God is Holy everything he does is righteous.

Genesis goes on to say that God did indeed fellowship with Adam for He told Adam personally **"... I have given you every herb bearing seed, which is upon the face of all the earth, and every tree, in the which *is* the fruit of a tree yielding seed; to you it shall be for meat."** (Gen 1:29). Genesis 2:19 also informs us that God also brought every fowl of the air and every beast of the field unto Adam to see what he would call them. Finally, in Genesis 3:8 we see that God walked in the Garden of Eden in the cool of the day to personally visit with Adam.

So, while the first man was righteous in God's eyes, man, by his own choice, forsook his God-given righteousness in order to become as god, i.e. knowing good and evil. Adam chose to know the way of the world as opposed to Jesus who is **"... the way ..."** (Jn 10:6). Adam chose to know the flesh whose life is in the blood rather than Jesus who is **"... the life ..."** (Jn 10:6) and Adam chose to know Satan the father of lies as opposed to Jesus who is **"... the truth ..."** (Jn 10:6). Can man then attain immortality by his own righteousness? Sinful man says YES but the Bible makes it very clear the answer is **NO!**

The Bible clearly illustrates that self-achieved righteousness is impossible. This is not because man is in incapable of being righteous, for we shown that man has such a capability. Rather man is incapable of regaining his lost righteousness by himself. This is due to his inherent sinful nature. In Genesis Chapter 4 we read that Adam and Eve bore two sons, Cain and

Able, and that; **"... in the process of time it came to pass, that Cain brought of the fruit of the ground an offering unto the LORD. And Abel, he also brought of the firstlings of his flock and of the fat thereof. And the LORD had respect unto Abel and to his offering: but unto Cain and to his offering he had not respect. And Cain was very wroth, and his countenance fell. And the Lord said unto Cain, Why art thou wroth, and why is thy countenance fallen? If thou doest well, shalt thou not be accepted? And if thou doest not well, sin lieth at the door..."** (Gen 4.3-7).

Here we have two brothers. Neither is said to have been involved in any unseemly behavior. Both have been raised by the same parents who knew God personally at one time. Each builds his own alter, one laden with beautiful fruits and fragrant flowers, the product of the worshipper's honorable toil, and the expression, no doubt of his grateful and sincere homage, the other is dripping with the blood of an innocent dead lamb. The difference between the two brothers did not consist in the superiority of either ones nature, for they were both **"... shapen in iniquity, and in sin did *their* mother conceive [them]."** (Psm 51:5). The difference was in the sacrifices that they presented to God.

Cain presented a self-righteous sacrifice, the work of his own hand and hence was rejected. Able, on the other hand, presented a righteous sacrifice, a Biblical atonement for his sin because **"... almost all things are by the law purged with blood; and without shedding of blood is no remission [of sin]"** (Heb 9:22), and consequently it was accepted. It was; **"By faith Able offered unto God a more excellent sacrifice than**

Cain, by which he obtained witness that he was righteous, God testifying of his gifts ..." (Heb 11.4). The offeror and the offering are inseparable. Both stand or fall together. God regards the offering in the light of the offeror, and proclaimed, even in that early age, man's self-righteousness cannot save him from the law of sin and death.

There are many other examples in the Old Testament that illustrate that righteousness can be obtained. In every instance, it entirely excludes man's self-righteousness as the ground upon which God pronounces the sentence of being righteousness. **"He that trusteth is his own heart is a fool ..."** (Prov 28:26) because **"... all our righteousness are as filthy rags ..."** (Isa 64:6).

In the Book of Philippians the Apostle Paul clearly presents the case that man's self-righteousness cannot provide salvation. Paul says that he himself was blameless **"... touching the righteousness which is in the law ..."** (Phil 3:6), and that he was **"... more exceedingly zealous of the traditions of his fathers"** (Gal 1:14) however in spite of all of outward self-righteousness he counted his own righteousness **"... as loss for the excellency of the knowledge of Christ Jesus my Lord ..."** and counted all things **"... but dung ..."** that he could win Christ, **"And be found in him, not having mine own righteousness, which is of the law, but that which is through the faith of Christ, the righteousness which is of God by faith:** (Phil 3:8).

Probably the most chilling account of God's utter contempt for mans self-righteousness is His destruction of the entire human race, excepting Noah and his family. Matthew 24:38 informs us **"... in the days before the** flood they were eating and drinking, marrying and giving in marriage ...". Now, none of these things are bad in and of themselves but when man does those things without keeping God in his knowledge "... **the works of the flesh are manifest, which are** *these*: **Adultery, fornication, uncleanness, lasciviousness, Idolatry, witchcraft, hatred, variance, emulations, wrath, strife, seditions, heresies, Envyings, murders, drunkenness, revellings, and such like ..."** (Gal 5:19-21). And so it was in Noah's day for; "... **God saw that the wickedness of man was great in the earth, and that every imagination of the thoughts of his [mans] heart was only evil continually"** (Gen 6:5) "... **behold, I will destroy them with the earth."** (Gen 6:13).

Even though God "... **is longsuffering to us-ward, not willing that any should perish, but that all should come to repentance."** (2 Pet 3:9) there comes a time when mans cup of iniquity becomes full to the brim and God executes judgment to stop the abominable behavior. One can discern from the conversation Abraham had with the LORD in Genesis 18:20-32 that there must be ten or more righteous people in a nation (or in the world) to stem God's judgment. The number ten in the Bible represents the perfection of divine order. Consequently, one may conclude that whenever the number of men that "... **love the Lord with all** *their* **heart, and all** *their* **soul, and all** *their* **might"** (Deut 6:5) dwindle to such a point that no revival to God's divine order is possible, judgment is executed. Fortunately for us, "... **Noah found grace in the eyes of the LORD"** because "... **Noah was a just man and perfect in his generations, and Noah walked with God."** (Gen 6:8-9).

Another example for our serious consideration is the kingdoms of Sodom and Gomorrah. Just prior to their destruction, the inhabitants of these kingdoms were doing what was right in their own eyes, they were self-righteous. Here again **"...in the days of Lot; they did eat, they drank, they bought, they sold, and they planted, they builded."** (Lk 17:28). Again not bad things in and of themselves but without God in their knowledge **"... the plowing [good, honest hard work] of the wicked is sin"** (Prov 21:4) and the same day Lot went out of Sodom **"... it rained fire and brimstone from heaven, and destroyed them all."** (Lk 17:29) because God could not find ten righteous men within the kingdoms. Self-righteousness on a personal level begets the judgment of God. Self-righteousness on a national level begets the judgment of God. Self-righteousness on a global level begets the judgment of God.

The Prophet Isaiah also provides a very somber warning against self-righteousness; **"They [the self-righteous] shall rest in their beds, each one walking in his uprightness [self-righteousness]. But draw near hither, ye sons of the sorceress, the seed of the adulterer and the whore. Against whom do ye sport yourselves? Against whom make ye a wide mouth, and draw out the tongue? Are ye not children of transgression, a seed of falsehood, Enflaming yourselves with idols under every green tree, slaying the children in the valleys under the clifts of the rocks? Among the smooth stones of the stream is thy portion; they, they are thy lot: even to them hast thou poured a drink offering, thou hast offered a meat offering. Should I receive comfort in these?**

Upon a lofty and high mountain hast thou set thy bed: even thither wentest thou up to offer sacrifice. Behind the doors also and the posts hast thou set up thy remembrance: for thou hast discovered thyself to another than me, and art gone up; thou hast enlarged thy bed, and made thee a covenant with them; thou lovest their bed where thou sawest it. And thou wentest to the king with ointment, and didst increase thy perfumes, and didst send thy messengers far off, and didst debase thyself even unto hell. Thou art wearied in the greatness of thy way; yet saidst thou not, There is no hope: thou hast found the life of thine hand; therefore thou wast not grieved. And of whom hast thou been afraid or feared, that thou hast lied, and hast not remembered me [God], nor laid it to thy heart? Have not I [God] held my peace even of old, and thou fearest me not? I will declare thy righteousness [self-righteousness], and thy works; for they shall not profit thee." (Isa 57:1-12). "... your iniquities [self-righteousness behavior] have separated between you and your God, and your sins have hid his face from you, that he will not hear. For your hands are defiled with blood, and your fingers with iniquity; your lips have spoken lies, your tongue hath muttered perverseness. None calleth for justice, nor any pleadeth for truth: they trust in vanity, and speak lies; they conceive mischief, and bring forth iniquity. The way of peace they know not; and there is no judgment in their goings: they have made them crooked paths: whosoever goeth therein shall not know peace." (Isa 58:1-4, 8). "...the wicked are like the troubled sea, when it cannot rest, whose waters cast up mire and dirt. There is no peace, saith my God, to the wicked." (Isa 57:20-21). "Know ye not that the unrighteous shall not inherit the kingdom of God? ..." (1 Cor 6:9).

Finally, God Himself gives a warning to the self-righteous: "Woe unto *them* that *are* wise in their own eyes, and prudent in their own sight!" (Isa 6:19) for "*There is* a generation *that are* pure in their own eyes, and *yet* is not washed from their filthiness." (Prov 30:12). "The way of the fool is right in his own eyes ..." (Prov 13:15). Why does God call the self-righteous fools? Because instead of comparing themselves to a Holy God, they compare themselves to other men. And, the easiest thing in the world to do is to find someone who is more outwardly sinful than yourself. Therefore take heed because, "... they measuring themselves by themselves, and comparing themselves among themselves, are not wise." (2 Cor 10:12). What little relative merit we may or may not have does not even enter into the picture of salvation because "... the scripture hath concluded all under sin ..." (Gal 3:22).

Consequently, the only conclusion on can come to is, due to man's sinful nature, ("The wicked are estranged from the womb: they go astray as soon as they be born, speaking lies." Psm 58:3) salvation via self-righteousness is impossible.

2. Righteousness By Keeping The Law

The next most popular belief is, *if I keep the law, God will consider me righteous.* Unfortunately, this too is a false premise because keeping the law is just a subset of attaining righteousness by being self-righteousness.

People who subscribe to this form of self-righteousness do it in the name of morality. However, since this is a very commonly held belief we will look at it in more depth.

When people say that one must keep the law in order to be saved they are referring to the Ten Commandments as enumerated in Exodus 20:1-17. The Ten Commandments are an expression of God's holy nature and the rule of action that God has laid down or assigned for the government of man in his relations to his Creator and his fellow-creatures.

As a refresher the *Ten Commandments* are as follows:

1. Thou shalt have no other gods before me
2. Thou shalt not make unto thee any graven image or any likeness of anything that is in heaven above, or that is in the earth beneath, or that is in the water under the earth: Thou shalt not bow down thyself to them, nor serve them
3. Thou shalt not take the name of the LORD thy God in vain
4. Remember the Sabbath day, to keep it holy
5. Honour thy father and thy mother
6. Thou shalt not kill
7. Thou shalt not commit adultery
8. Thou shalt not steal
9. Thou shalt not bear false witness against thy neighbor
10. Thou shalt not covet thy neighbour's house, nor his manservant, nor his maidservant, nor his ox, nor his ass, nor any thing that is thy neighbour's

In a nutshell, the misconception that people have

regarding this way of attaining a righteous state with God is they think that if they outwardly keep the law to what they say is the best of their ability, God will see that they are trying hard to be a good moral person, and having done more good than bad in their life (by their own assessment), God will consider them righteous and allow them to enter into the glories of Heaven.

Paul the Apostle makes statements to the effect that he kept the law outwardly from birth but was still considered guilty before an almighty God. Paul was a **"...Pharisee, the son of a Pharisee ..."**, lived according the most strict sect of the Pharisees and **"... as touching the righteousness which is in the law, *he was* blameless."** (Acts 23:5-6). Furthermore, he said that such things were of no gain to him but rather **"... counted them but dung ..."** (Phil 3:5, 8). It can then be concluded that those who do depend upon keeping the law for obtaining righteousness, are really **"... the enemies of the cross of Christ: whose end is destruction, whose God is their belly, and whose glory is in their shame ..."** (Phil 3:18-19).

You may ask, if the keeping the law does not make you righteous, why then was the law given? The law was given because of mans transgressions. It was given to give sin the character of transgression. It was given to define sin and to reveal the sin in man. Paul says **"... I had not known sin, [that is the nature of sin] but by the law: for I had not known lust, except the law had said, Thou shalt not covet."** (Rom 7:7) for **"... by the law is the knowledge of sin."** (Rom 3:20). He went on to say **"Moreover the law entered [at Mt. Sinai], that the offence [offensiveness of sin] might abound [be**

openly revealed]…" (Rom 5:20).

The law **"… was our schoolmaster *to bring us unto Christ."** (Gal 3:24). The law boxed man into a corner and forced him to see himself as God sees him, a wicked sinner. The law was given to convict us of our sinfulness and lead us to repentance. Contemplating the law and extrapolating its edicts and precepts out their fullest extent is humbling and alters one's perception of self. It leads one to the right and proper conclusion, namely, man is not one bit righteous and the only hope of avoiding the damnation of Hell is for a Saviour to save your rebellious and wicked soul from the punishment it justly deserves. The law brought man face to face with the true Holiness of God and the truth that; **"… everyone of us shall give account of himself to God."** (Rom 12:14).

Before we were saved, before we put our faith trust in the Lord Jesus Christ, God's law condemned us. **"Before faith came, we were kept under the law, shut up unto the faith which should afterwards be revealed."** (Gal 3:23). We were subject to God's law of sin and death, yet unable to live up to its exacting demands due to our sin nature. It did not matter whether we knew the written law or not for God's law is written in every man's conscience; **"…when the Gentiles, which have not the law, do by nature the things contained in the law, these, having not the law, are a law unto themselves: Which shew the work of the law written in their hearts, their conscience also bearing witness …"** (Rom 2:14-15). Because man is conceived in sin and born in iniquity the law **"… concluded all under sin …"** (Gal 3:22). God's final verdict – **"… all have** sinned, and come short of the glory of God" (Rom 3:23) and man has nothing to say on his own behalf because, due to the law, **"… every mouth may be stopped …"** (Rom 3:19) and God **"… will by no means clear *the guilty* …"** (Ex 34:7). God knew that the whole world stood condemned before Him and that is why **"… when the fullness of time was come, God sent forth his Son, made of a woman, made under the law, To redeem them that were under the law, that we might receive the adoption of sons."** (Gal 4:4).

When exactly was the fullness of time? Well, Jesus came at the height of Israel's strict outward adherence to the law. Israel was an occupied country at the time of Christ. They were under Roman rule and dominion in the time that is referred to as the Pax Romana (27 B.C. to 180 A.D.), or the Roman Peace. All regional warring had ceased, a general peace was enforced throughout the Roman Empire and trade flourished. It was during this time of tranquility and relative ease that the scribes and Pharisees implemented a most rigorous adherence to the outward requirements of the law.

They thought that by keeping the exact letter of the law, down to the minutest detail, they were complying with the full intent of the law. They thought that because they interpreted the requirements of the law in the most conservative and restrictive way possible, they were righteous. However, they were in reality just damning themselves and others to Hell because salvation comes **"Not by works of righteousness [keeping the law] which we have done, but according to his [God's] mercy he [God] saved us, by the washing of regeneration, and renewing of the Holy Ghost;"** (Tit

3:5).

Jesus bluntly points out the hypocrisy of their ritualism and misguided adherence to the law; "**... The scribes and the Pharisees sit in Moses' seat: All therefore whatsoever they bid you observe, *that* observe and do; but do not ye after their works: for they say and do not. . ... Woe unto you, scribes and Pharisees, hypocrites! for ye shut up the kingdom of heaven against men: for ye neither go *in yourselves*, neither suffer ye them that are entering to go in. ... Woe unto you, scribes and Pharisees, hypocrites! for ye compass sea and land to make one proselyte, and when he is made, ye make him twofold more the child of hell than yourselves.**" (Matt 23:23-33).

The irony was that while they thought they were keeping the law to its most minute and exacting detail they were in reality, grossly violating the purpose and intent of the law, namely to show them their need of a Saviour. Jesus Christ himself describes the lengths the scribes and Pharisees went to make themselves appear righteous under the guise of keeping the law and what His assessment was of their efforts; "**...they bind heavy burdens and grievous to be borne, and lay *them* on men's shoulders; but they themselves will not move them with one of their fingers. But all their works they do for to be seen of men [self-righteousness]: they make broad their phylacteries, and enlarge the borders of their garments [wear extravagant cloths to be more noticed], And love the uppermost rooms at feasts, and the chief seats in the synagogues, and greetings in the markets, and to be called of men Rabbi, Rabbi [want special recognition for their** position in society]. But be not ye called Rabbi: for one is your Master, *even* Christ; and all ye are brethren. ... Neither be ye called masters: for one is your Master, *even* Christ. But he that is greatest among you shall be your servant. And whosoever shall exalt himself shall be abased; and he that shall humble himself shall be exalted. ... Woe unto you, scribes and Pharisees, hypocrites! for ye devour widows' houses, and for a pretence make long prayer: therefore ye shall receive the greater damnation. ... *Ye* blind guides, which say, Whosoever shall swear by the temple, it is nothing; but whosoever shall swear by the gold of the temple, he is a debtor! *Ye* fools and blind: for whether is greater, the gold, or the temple that sanctifieth the gold? And Whosoever shall swear by the alter, it is nothing; but whosoever sweareth by the gift that is upon it, he is guilty. *Ye* fools and blind: for whether is greater, the gift, or the altar, sweareth by it, and by all things thereon. And whoso shall swear by the temple, sweareth by it, and by him that dwelleth therein. And he that shall swear by heaven, sweareth by the throne of God, and by him that sitteth thereon. Woe unto you, scribes and Pharisees, hypocrites! For ye pay tithe of mint and anise and cumin, and have omitted the weightier *matters* of the law, judgment, mercy, and faith: these ought ye to have done, and not to leave the other undone. *Ye* blind guides, which strain at a gnat, and swallow a camel. Woe unto you, scribes and Pharisees, hypocrites! For ye make clean the outside of the cup and of the platter, but within they are full of extortion and excess. *Thou* blind Pharisee, cleanse first that which is within the cup, and platter, that the outside of them may be clean also. Woe unto you, scribes and Pharisees, hypocrites! For ye are like unto whited sepulchers, which indeed appear beautiful outward, but are within full of dead man's bones, and of all uncleanness. Even so ye also outwardly appear righteous unto men, but within ye are full of hypocrisy and iniquity. Woe unto you, scribes and Pharisees, hypocrites! Because ye build the tombs of the prophets, and garnish the sepulchers of the righteous, and say If we had been in the days of our fathers, we would not have been partakers with them in the blood of the prophets. Wherefore ye be witnesses unto yourselves, that ye are the children of them which killed the prophets. Fill ye up then the measure of your fathers. *Ye* serpents, *ye* generation of vipers, how can ye escape the damnation of hell?"** (Matt 23:4-33).

The Pharisees thought they were so righteous that they had the audacity to declare themselves so in their prayers; **"The Pharisee stood and prayed thus with himself, God, I thank thee, that I am not as other men are, extortioners, unjust, adulterers, or even as this publican. I fast twice in the week, I give tithes of all that I possess."** (Lk 18:11-12). By declaring themselves to be righteous (i.e. equal to God), they were in reality just sealing their own doom because only the LORD is righteous; **"Righteous *art* thou, O LORD, and upright *are* thy judgments. Thy testimonies *that* thou has commanded *are* righteous and very faithful. Thy righteousness *is* an everlasting righteousness, and thy law *is* the truth. The righteousness of thy testimonies** *is* **everlasting: ..."** (Ps 119:137-138,142,144).

Jesus drives this point home when He declared that a publican **"standing afar off, [that] would not lift up so much as *his* eyes unto heaven, but smote upon his breast, saying, God be merciful to me a sinner."** (Lk 18:13) was **"justified [declared righteous]** *rather* **than the other [the Pharisee]: for every one that exalteth himself shall be abased; and he that humbleth himself shall be exalted."** (Lk 18:14).

It is also important to note that Satan promised man that; **"... your eyes shall be opened, and ye shall be as gods, knowing good and evil."** (Gen 3:5) and sure enough, one of the side effects of sin is people perceive themselves to be godly. Therefore, it should come as no surprise that the Pharisees behaved as all demigods do, elevating and aggrandizing themselves while having nothing but distain for others. Without a doubt their eyes were wide open, just as Satan said they would be but, **"... who** *is* **blind as** *he that is* **perfect, ..."** (Isa 42:19).

So it can be rightfully concluded, righteousness comes only through faith in Jesus Christ. Nothing you can say or do can make you righteous. No one can be declared righteous by keeping the law for the law demands perfection of life and character that no mortal can attain. We, at best, only think that we observe the law and the sad fact is that this belief is at best just a wishful tradition taught by man, and at worst a sure prescription for eternal damnation. Remember, **"All the ways of a man are clean in his own eyes; but the LORD weigheth the spirits."** (Prov. 16:2).

3. Righteousness By Religion

The third most popular belief is, *if I am religious, God will consider me righteous.* This group of people insist that god, is god, is God, and whatever name people choose to call God by doesn't really matter. They say that what really matters is, is that you are sincere and faithful in your worship and if you are, God will consider you righteous.

They intellectualize that it is ridiculous to believe that God could be so narrow minded as to restrict salvation to just one way, especially in light of the multitude of cultures and customs in the world. Unfortunately, this line of logic leads its adherents straight into the flames of Hell, so be advised of the old adage; *education without salvation is damnation.* The facts they refuse to accept are;

1. There is in reality one and only one God and if **"Thou believest that there is one God; thou doest well: the devils also believe, and tremble."** (Jam 2:19).
2. True salvation is through one person and only one person, and that person is Jesus Christ for **"Neither is there salvation in any other: for there is none other name under heaven given among men, where we must be saved."** (Acts 4:12).

Whether you agree with this fact or not, the way of salvation is extremely narrow. Jesus himself let us know this, and that is why He said, **"Enter ye in at the strait gate: for wide is the gate, and broad is the way, that leadeth to destruction, and many there be which go in thereat: Because strait is the gate, and narrow is the way, which leadeth unto life, and few there be**

that find it." (Matt 7:13-14).

In fact the way is so narrow that only through the person of Jesus Christ can one enter into the presence of God and that is why **"Jesus saith unto him, I am the way, the truth, and the life: no man cometh unto the Father but by me."** (Jn 14:6). Jesus and only Jesus has been **"... ordained of God *to be* the Judge of quick and dead. To him give all the prophets witness, that through his name whosoever believeth in him shall receive remission of sins."** (Acts 10:42-43).

Jesus is the one and only way to Glory, there is no other way. God states this very clearly in Jeremiah 32:39 **"... I [God] will give them [man] one heart, and one way [Jesus Christ], that they may fear me for ever, for the good of them, and of their children after them:"** Unless you accept Jesus Christ as your Lord and Saviour, you will likewise perish in the flames of Hell. No amount of baptisms, prayers, financial contributions, acts of goodwill, homage, genuflecting, self-denial, self-flagellation, self-mutilation, sacrifices (animal or human), adherence and execution of any kind of man derived doctrine, rights, or practices can make one righteousness in the eyes of God.

Jesus is the one and only way to God. This means you must be in Jesus and the only way to be in Jesus is to be spiritually baptized into His body via the act of salvation. The reason one can be so emphatic that Jesus is the only to enter into the presence of God is, no other religion other than Biblical Christianity has absolute, infallible and corroborated proof of its truth, namely a risen Saviour. **"... Christ died for our sins according to the scriptures; And that he as buried,**

and that he rose again the third day according to the scriptures; And that he was seen of Cephas, then of the twelve: After that, he was seen of above five hundred brethren at once ..." (1 Cor 15:3-6) because as Jesus himself said, **"... I am the resurrection, and the life: he that believeth in me, though he were dead, yet shall he live: and whosoever liveth and believeth in me shall never die..."** (Jn 11:25-26).

You might ask why Jesus was only seen by believers after His resurrection. The Apostle Luke provides a very perceptive answer by pointing out that; **"... If they hear not Moses and the prophets, neither will they be persuaded, though one rose from the dead."** (Luke 16:31). Consequently, if anyone chooses to remain willingly ignorant of Biblical salvation, Jesus says you should **"Let them alone: ... And if the blind lead the blind, both shall fall into the ditch."** (Matt 15:14).

4. Righteousness By Faith

The one and only way God will declare you righteous is by **"... [believing] the record that God gave of his Son."** (1 Jn 5:10), i.e. the Gospel. One becomes righteous by receiving the righteousness of Christ by faith and by faith alone because; **"...by grace are ye saved through faith; and that not of yourselves: it is the gift of God: Not of works, lest any man boast."** (Eph 2:8-9). Remember; **"... *there* is no God else beside me; a just God and a Saviour; *there is* none beside me. Look unto me [have faith] and be ye saved, all the ends of the earth: for I *am* God, and *there is* none else.** (Isa 45:21-22).

What is faith? The Apostle Paul defines it for us

in Hebrews 11:1; **"...faith is the substance [ground or confidence] of things hoped for, the evidence of things not seen."** In other words, *faith* is *dependence upon the veracity of another.* Faith takes God at His word without any *if's*, *and's* or *but's*. If the King James Bible says it, believe it, because God's word is infinitely powerful; **"So shall my [God's] word be that goeth forth out of my [God's] mouth: it shall not return unto me void, but it shall accomplish that which I please, and it shall prosper *in the thing* whereto I sent it."** (Isa 55:11).

Faith is all important if you wish to stand in the presence of God because, **"...without faith it is impossible to please [God] ..."** (Heb 11:6). Abraham verified that **"... The just shall live by faith."** (Rom 1:17) because **"... Abraham believed God, and it was imputed unto him for righteousness: and he was called a Friend of God."** (Jam 2:23).

God justifies those who place their faith in the finished work of Jesus Christ and declares them righteous. By faith and by faith alone can God impute righteousness to your soul because your **"... righteousness is of me, saith the LORD."** (Isa 54:17).

Salvation is nigh to you this very moment as **"... The word is nigh thee, *even* in thy mouth, and in thy heart: that is, the word of faith, which we preach;"** (Rom 10:8). All you have to do to receive it in all its completeness is to **"... believe the record that God gave of his Son."** (1 Jn 5:10).

Your soul is declared righteous by being redeemed by Jesus Christ Himself. The word *redeemed* means *to deliver by the payment of a ransom*; and we know that Jesus paid the ransom for our souls because the **"... the Son of man came.... To give his life a ransom for many."** (Matt 20:28).

Jesus had to redeem us from the law of sin and death because the law could not make us righteous in that it was weak through the flesh. Obeying the law to the best of our ability could not make us righteousness: not because the law is imperfect, but because man is imperfect. Due to mans sinfulness, God had mercy on mankind and sent His own Son to pay the sin debt for us. And; **"... now the righteousness of God without the law is manifested, being witnessed by the law and the prophets; even the righteousness of God *which is* by faith of Jesus Christ unto all, and upon all them that believe ..."** (Rom 3:21-22).

The law has not been set aside, it has been honored, obeyed, and satisfied, in every jot and tittle of its claims upon the believer, because **"Christ hath redeemed us from the curse of the law, being made a curse for us ..."** (Gal 3:13). This is why the Psalmist exclaimed; **"...He shall receive the blessing from the LORD, and righteousness from the God of his salvation."** (Psm 24:3, 5). **"Mercy and truth are met together; righteousness and peace have kissed *each other*. Truth shall spring out of the earth; and righteousness shall look down from heaven."** (Psm 85:10, 11).

Faith is an individual thing; repentance is an individual thing; and salvation is an individual thing. It is important to note that each person has to look to the Lord Jesus Christ for himself. No one can look to the Lord Jesus Christ for another; **"... every man shall be put to death for his own sin."** (Deut 24:16). Remember

"The soul that sinneth, it shall die. The son shall not bear the iniquity of the father, neither shall the father bear the iniquity of the son: the righteousness of the righteous shall be upon him, and the wickedness of the wicked shall be upon him. (Ez 18:20).

The good news is; **"… if the wicked will turn from all his sins that he hath committed, and keep all my statutes, and do that which is lawful and right, he shall surely live, he shall not die. All his transgressions that he hath committed, they shall not be mentioned unto him: in his righteousness that he hath done he shall live."** (Ez 18:21-22). It is easy, all one has to do is to repent, look in faith to the author and finisher of our faith, and live for **"… whosoever believeth in Him shall not perish, but have everlasting life"**. Placing one's faith in Jesus Christ is the one and only way by which God deems us righteous.

Before one can look to Jesus in faith a person must fully realize their lost and hopeless condition. Their heart must be "pricked" by the Holy Ghost and experience the Godly sorrow that worketh repentance. They must realize they are just one heartbeat away from the damnation of Hell. They must realize their own righteousness is as filthy rags to God and "keeping" the law is the path to certain damnation as is reliance on religion. They must realize how sinful they really are in the eyes of a thrice Holy God and confess that they are a wicked sinner. It is then and only then that calling on the name of the Lord for the salvation of their soul, will they receive forgiveness of their sins. Remember; **"… except ye repent ye shall all likewise perish."** (Lk 13:3), **"… a man is justified by faith without the deeds**

of the law." (Rom 3:28) and **"we have redemption through his [Jesus'] blood, the forgiveness of sins ..."** (Eph 1:7).

It is also very important to understand that there is a world of difference between a profession of faith and a confession unto faith. It is the difference of going to Heaven or Hell. A profession of faith (acknowledgement of Jesus as the Son of God) may appease the conscience and provide a religious experience, but all Jesus will ever say to you is **"... I never knew you: depart from me, ye that work iniquity."** (Matt 7:23). A confession unto faith (repenting of your sins and accepting Jesus Christ as your Lord and Master in fear and trembling) redeems your soul and Jesus shall say to you **"... Well done, *thou* good and faithful servant ...enter thou into the joy of thy lord."** (Matt 25:21).

Salvation

One might now be thinking, I understand that righteousness comes through faith in Jesus Christ and not by claiming self-righteousness, trying to keep the law or adhering to religious dogmas. But I am still unsure how righteousness plays into the plan of salvation?

Being declared righteous is of supreme importance to one's salvation. If your soul is righteous at the time of death, it will be able to enter into God's presence and will receive a new immortal body. Conversely, if your soul is not righteous at the time of death, or said another way, if you are not justified in God's sight, you cannot enter into the presence of God and your soul will be cast into Hell.

Along with a conscience God also provided man a

measure of faith. **"For by grace are ye saved through faith; and that [faith is] not of yourselves [the measure of faith you have is not a result of your own efforts]: it [your faith] is the gift of God:"** (Eph 2:8). Said another way; every man is born with a knowledge of God and a measure of faith. This knowledge of the truth and its associated faith is **"... the law written in their [mans] hearts, their conscience also bearing witness ..."** (Rom 2:15).

Man also has the free will to place this God-given faith on whomever he believes can make him righteous before God thereby atoning for his sins that he knows he has committed via his conscience. Some people choose to place their faith in themselves, attempting to atone for their sins through self-righteousness. Others place their faith in their ability to atone for their sins through keeping the law or by religious practices. The wise place their faith back on the provider of their faith, namely Jesus Christ.

When the Holy Spirit pricks a person's heart it causes Godly sorrow and brings home the realization that you truly are a sinner, having sinned against God's Holy law and deserve the punishment for doing so. This Godly sorrow causes one to repent or to forsake their god, pride, self-righteousness and sinful ways. The pricking of the heart also drives one to their knees as they realize their hopeless condition and causes them to call on the name of the Lord for the salvation of their wicked soul, acknowledging Jesus Christ as their new Lord and Master. Therefore the wise, knowing they are a sinner and deserve punishment believe the Gospel, namely; **"... that Christ died for our sins according to** the scriptures; And that he was buried, and that he rose again the third day according to the scriptures." (1 Cor 15:3-4).

I believe it is best to audibly call on the Lord to save your soul from the damnation of Hell instead of thinking the thought. I believe a spoken request for salvation is to be preferred over a silent one because it confirms and proclaims the heart's true desire. Joel 2:32 says "… it shall come to pass, *that* whosoever shall call on the name of the LORD shall be delivered:…", Acts 2:21 and Romans 10:13 both say "… whosoever shall call on the name of the Lord shall be saved." and *call* means *to utter a loud sound, to utter the name, to utter with a loud voice* and *utter* means *to speak.* Salvation is only available to living mortal man and just like in our work-a-day world, if you want something you have to ask for it. Everyone knows that wishing and desiring does not necessarily get you what you want.

Audibly calling on the Lord tames the tongue, which "… *is* an unruly evil, full of deadly poison," (Jam 3:8), "… it defileth the whole body, and setteth on fire the course of nature; and it is set on fire of hell." (Jam 3:6). Having the tongue audibly pronounce Jesus as your Saviour and having the tongue unequivocally proclaim Jesus Christ as your new Lord and Master extinguishes its Hell-fire.

Upon placing one's faith in Christ, your soul is spiritually baptized into the body of Christ. And because you are now part of the spiritual body of Christ, your sins are paid for via Christ's shed blood and death on the cross. Christ's righteousness is now imputed to you. Christ paid your sin debt and you are therefore free from any vestige of sin. You are now righteous in the sight of God. **"Therefore if any man be in Christ, he is a new creature: old things are passed away; behold, all things are become new. All things are of God, who hath reconciled us to himself by Jesus Christ, and hath given to us the ministry of reconciliation; To wit, that God was in Christ, reconciling the world unto himself, not imputing their trespasses unto them; and hath committed unto us the word of reconciliation. ... For he [God] hath made him [Jesus] to be sin for us, who knew no sin [he is righteous]; that we might be made the righteousness of God in him."** (2 Cor 6:19-21). **"...by him [Jesus] all that believe are justified from all things, from which ye could not be justified by the law of Moses."** (Acts 13:39). **"Therefore being justified [declared righteous] by faith, we have peace with God through our Lord Jesus Christ: By whom also we have access by faith into this grace wherein we stand, and rejoice in hope of the glory of God."** (Rom 5:1). Because our sins are washed away **"... the peace of God, which passeth all understanding, shall keep your hearts and minds through Jesus Christ."** (Phil 4:7).

The believer may know, on the sure testimony of God, that all this is true because God cannot lie; **"God *is* not a man, that he should lie; neither the son of man, that he should repent [change His mind]: hath he said, and shall he not do *it*? or hath he spoken, and shall he not make it good?"** (Num 23:19). The act of faith in Jesus Christ to be your all-sufficient Saviour requires confidence in the fact that **"... God sent his only begotten Son into the world, that we might live** through him." (1 Jn 4:9).

Remember; "God commendeth his live toward us, in that, while we were yet sinners, Christ died for us." (Rom 5:8). "For God so loved the world, that he gave his only begotten Son, that whosoever believeth in him should not perish, but have everlasting life. For God sent not his Son into the world to condemn the world; but that the world through him might be saved. He that believeth on him is not condemned: but he that believeth not is condemned already, because he hath not believed in the name of the only begotten Son of God." (Jn 3:16-18).

Bloody Covenant

"And when Abram was ninety years old and nine, the LORD appeared to Abram, and said unto him, I am the Almighty God; walk before me, and be thou perfect. And I will make my covenant between me and thee, and will multiply thee exceedingly. And Abram fell on his face: and God talked with him, saying, As for me, behold, my covenant is with thee, and thou shalt be a father of many nations. Neither shall thy name any more be called Abram, but thy name shall be Abraham; for a father of many nations have I made thee. And I will make thee exceeding fruitful, and I will make nations of thee, and kings shall come out of thee. And I will establish my covenant between me and thee and thy seed after thee in their generations for an everlasting covenant, to be a God unto thee, and to thy seed after thee. And I will give unto thee, and to thy seed after thee, the land wherein thou art a stranger, all the land of

Canaan, for an everlasting possession; and I will be their God. And God said unto Abraham, Thou shalt keep my covenant therefore, thou, and thy seed after thee in their generations. This is my covenant, which ye shall keep, between me and you and thy seed after thee; Every man child among you shall be circumcised. And ye shall circumcise the flesh of your foreskin; and it shall be a token of the covenant betwixt me and you." (Gen 17:1-12).

The covenant of circumcision served as a sign, seal, and token of the Old Covenant and separated Abraham and his posterity, according to the flesh, from the rest of mankind. It was the seal of Abraham's justification by faith; **"And he received the sign of circumcision, a seal of the righteousness of the faith which he *had yet* being uncircumcised: that he might be the father of all them that believe,"** (Rom 4:11) and God's pledge that He would bless Abraham. It would be through Abraham and his seed that God would eventually bless all the nations and families on Earth.

This covenant of circumcision applied only to males because a person's blood is received from their father. It is because the male element produces life, and the fact that **"... the man is not of the woman; but the woman of the man. Neither was the man created for the woman; but the woman for the man."** (1 Cor 11:8-9) that the covenant of circumcision applied only to males. Not being able to generate life blood in or by themselves, females were therefore exempted from being circumcised.

The blood shed during the procedure also served as a real and powerful reminder that without Christ shedding His blood as an atonement for our sins the putting off the flesh would be impossible. **"For we are the circumcision who worship God in the spirit, and rejoice in Christ Jesus, and have no confidence in the flesh."** (Phil 3:3). **"For in him [Christ] dwelleth all the fullness of the Godhead bodily. And ye are complete in him, who is the head of all principality and power: in whom, also, ye are circumcised with the circumcision made without hands, in putting of the body of the sins of the flesh by the circumcision of Christ; buried with him in baptism; wherein, also, ye are risen with *him* through the faith of the operation of God, who hath raised him from the dead."** (Col 2:9-12). **"In whom [Christ] ye also *trusted*, after that ye heard the word of truth, the Gospel of your salvation; in whom also, after that ye believed, ye were sealed with that Holy Spirit of promise, which is the earnest of our inheritance, until the redemption of the purchased possession, unto the praise of his glory."** (Eph 1:13-14).

It also served as a reminder that salvation is only performed once. It was a one-time act that is forever and irreversible, hence the old saying, *once saved always saved*; **"... whatsoever God doeth, it shall be for ever: nothing can be put to it, nor any thing taken from it: and God doeth *it*, that *men* should fear before him."** (Ecc 3:14).

It can also be discerned that circumcision of the flesh was a picture of the Holy Ghost circumcising the heart at the time of salvation; **"... circumcision *is that* of the heart, in the spirit,..."** (Rom 2:29). Upon repenting and receiving the LORD Jesus Christ as your

Saviour the Holy Ghost circumcises your heart. He cuts off the sin crust that veils the heart and the blood of Christ washes it away. In the Bible this is referred to as the **"... circumcision made without hands ..."** thereby **"... putting off the body of sins of the flesh by the circumcision of Christ:** (Col 2:11). This bloody operation forever frees your soul from the enslavement of the lust of the eyes, the lust of the flesh, and the pride of life. And the Holy Ghost is able to perform this operation because; **"... the word of God is quick, and powerful, and sharper than any two-edged sword, piercing even to the dividing asunder of soul and spirit ..."** (Heb 4:12).

The circumcision of the heart is one's proof positive you are saved. The excising of the heart's sin crust results in a peace which passeth all understanding because the burden of sin has been removed. The result of this Divine operation is that it should be readily apparent to even the most casual observer that you are separated from the world, different and distinct, to the same degree that circumcision of the flesh attested to fact that one was a descendant of Abraham. Circumcision provided a clear, unambiguous, and graphic testimony of their faith in God's promised redemption and that suffering for a season was worth it in light of the full possession and enjoyment of the eternal inheritance that is received as a free gift by faith. **"Circumcise therefore the foreskin of your heart [sin crust that veils the sinner's heart], and be no more stiffnecked. For the LORD your God is God of gods, and Lord of lords, a great God, a mighty, and a terrible, which regardeth not persons, nor taketh reward:"** (Deut 10:16-17).

Bloody Sacrifice

"For Sarah conceived, and bare Abraham a son in his old age, at the set time of which God had spoken to him. … And Abraham was an hundred years old, when his son Isaac was born unto him." (Gen 21:2-5). And God said; "… Take now thy son, thine only son Isaac, whom thou lovest, and get thee into the land of Moriah; and offer him there for a burnt offering upon one of the mountains which I will tell thee of. … And they came to the place which God had told him of; and Abraham built an altar there, and laid the wood in order, and bound Isaac his son, and laid him on the altar upon the wood. And Abraham stretched forth his hand, and took the knife to slay his son. And the angel of the LORD called unto him out of heaven, and said, Abraham, Abraham: and he said, Here *am* I. And he said, Lay not thine hand upon the lad, neither do thou any thing unto him: for now I know that thou fearest God, seeing thou hast not withheld thy son, thine only son from me.

And Abraham lifted up his eyes, and looked, and behold behind *him* a ram caught in a thicket by his horns: and Abraham went and took the ram, and offered him up for a burnt offering in the stead of his son." (Gen 22: 2, 9-13).

Through this incident God made it clear, that a man would have to have an intercessor between sinful man and a righteous God. There would have to be a man capable of being the Saviour of the human race if anyone was to be saved. It showed that sinful flesh cannot make atonement for anything but rather an innocent substitute was required until the Saviour would arrive in the fullness of time. From the Garden of Eden until Christ shed His blood on the cross of Calvary, a substitute animal sacrifice was required in mans stead for the atonement of sin.

It also points out that God does not permit or sanction human sacrifice. This was a tremendous, but unappreciated, blessing to mankind. One can only imagine the horror, persecution and religious perversions that would have ensued had man been allowed to atone for his sin via the sacrifice of another.

Only innocent substitute animals were acceptable sacrifices, and God Himself would provide them, as He did the ram. The ram was a pledge of our expiation. When Christ shed His blood on the cross, He not only atoned for our sins but also became the propitiation for our sins, hence animal sacrifices were no longer needed because our sin debt was paid in full.

It is also important to note that all covenants were ratified by a sacrifice. Abraham's obedience to God was duly noted and rewarded. While the ram he had sacrificed was still burning on the alter, God renewed and ratified His covenant him, namely; **"… because thou hast done this thing, and has not withheld thy son, thine only *son*. That in blessing I will bless thee, and in multiplying, I will multiply thy seed as the stars of the heaven, and as the sand which *is* upon the sea shore; and thy seed shall possess the gate of his enemies;"** (Gen 22:16-17).

God promised that Abraham would have offspring as numerous as the stars of heaven and God, true to His word, proclaimed Abraham's spiritual seed are all those who have faith in God, i.e. *the saved*. Abraham's offspring would also be spiritually victorious. This will come to pass by the believer's faith, for by their faith they will overcome the world, and triumph over all the powers of darkness. Truly, we are more than conquerors and as such **"... we, being delivered out of the hand of our enemies, might serve him without fear."** (Lk 4:3). This is one reason why only Christians can say **"O death, where** *is* **they sting? O grave, where** *is* **thy victory?"** (1 Cor 15:55).

Golden Calf

Another striking illustration which will set forth the truth that sin must be paid for by blood is in the atonement which Moses offered after the people had broken God's law by the making of a golden calf at Mt. Sinai. Moses and Joshua had been on the mountain for forty days and forty nights. During their absence, Israel had given them up for dead. They demanded that Aaron construct a god to lead them on their way. The result was the manufacture of a golden calf. When Moses descended from the Mount with the Tablets of the Testimony in his hand he found Israel had already broken the first law of God's commands and were already cursed of God. Moses knew that nothing but a blood atonement could avert annihilation for the children of Israel. To remedy the situation Moses devised a unique dual-purpose atonement for Israel's sin. He showed Israel that blood is the only atonement for sin and blood is to be more valued than gold.

To effect atonement for their sin and to bring home the futility and uselessness of their gold and self-created god, Moses had each Israelite drink a bloody cup of indignation. **"And he took the calf which they had made, and burnt** *it* **in the fire, and ground** *it* **to powder, and strawed** *it* **upon the water, and made the children of Israel drink** *of it***."** (Ex 32:20). **"And I took your sin, the calf which ye had made, and burnt it with fire, and stamped it,** *and* **ground** *it* **very small,** *even* **until it was as small as dust: and I cast the dust thereof into the brook that descended out of the mount."** (Deut 9:21).

Moses was versed in art of alchemy for he **"... was learned in all the wisdom of the Egyptians, and was mighty in words and in deeds."** (Acts 7:22). Utilizing this knowledge Moses took the golden calf, melted it and removed the dross. The pure gold was then stamped, reducing it to thin foil sheets. The gold foil was then easily ground as fine as dust, thereby reducing it to 7-micron sized particles. The 7-micron sized particles were the exact same size as red blood cells, and the number 7 represents perfection, consequently the symbolism of Christ' perfect and sinless blood cannot go unnoticed in Moses' atonement.

Gold is insoluble in water and with a specific gravity of 19.5, is nineteen times heavier than water. Scientific experimentation has also proven that gold can be ground to less than 4 microns in diameter, so 7 micron sized particles would be an easy thing to make. At diameters of 10-microns and less, gold loses its golden color and actually becomes red in color, and so blood red colored water can easily be achieved by a solution of 7-micron sized gold particles suspended in water. Such a solution is referred to as a colloidal solution. The blood red colloidal solution was nontoxic and antibacterial, hence was a fitting substitute for the blood of the Lord Jesus Christ.

The red colored gold dust was then cast into the brook making the water blood red. This blood-red solution was taken by Moses before the Lord and presented to Him as an atonement for their sin; **"And it came to pass on the morrow, that Moses said unto the people. Ye have sinned a great sin: and now I will go up unto the Lord; peradventure I shall make an atonement for your sin. And Moses returned unto the Lord, and said, Oh, this people have sinned a great sin, and have made them gods of gold. Yet now, if thou wilt forgive their sin ---; and if not blot me, I pray thee, out of thy book which thou hast written."** (Ex 32:30-32).

Moses presented his atonement, saying, **"...peradventure I shall make an atonement for your sin."** The Lord saw the blood substitute, a fit type of the blood of the Lord Jesus Christ and adequate punishment for people who made an idol. God's wrath was averted, justice was served and fellowship restored. It is important to realize that while Christ died for the sin of the whole world and He tasted death for every man, it still remains a stubborn fact that only those who repent and accept the blood sacrifice that was made on their behalf will have their sins washed away and be saved from the damnation of Hell.

Atonement

Animal sacrifices were designed to lead a person to the understanding that they were sinners in need of a Saviour. They were intended to be expressions of thanksgiving and gratitude to God and were expiatory because without the shedding of blood there has never been remission of any kind of sin. The pardon procured by these offerings was only temporary and symbolical. **"For it is not possible that the blood of bulls and of goats should take away sins."** (Heb 10:4). And hence it is evident that the main design of these offerings was to adumbrate and illustrate the nature, necessity and efficacy of the sacrifice of Christ.

To the Hell-bound sinner the bloody offerings of are nothing more than the gruesome practices of a slaughterhouse religion. They point to the tens of thousands of gallons of blood that has been shed through the years, all to no seeming avail because men continue to wax worse and worse. What these folks fail to seize upon is the cornerstone of immortality, namely: without the shedding of blood, there is no remission of sin. And why must this be so? Because God's civil code says that if a man sins, the blood of a perfect man must be shed as atonement. And why must this so? Because the God of all creation, in His infinite wisdom, ordained it so. However, for those who still question, remember that **"... [God] giveth not account of any of his matters."** (Job 33:13).

Burnt Offering

The oldest, and most comprehensive of all the legal sacrifices is the burnt offering. This personal offering served as acknowledgement that the offeror was a sinner and required a sinless substitute to shed its blood on his behalf as payment for their sins. It was first performed by God himself as atonement for Adam's sin. Down through the ages, from Able onwards, it was performed by all who believed that someday the Lord would send a Redeemer. By this sacrifice they expressed their belief that the LORD would send His sinless Son to shed His blood for the remission of their sins. This is why the sacrifice had to be a male without blemish. It could be a bullock, a ram, a goat, a dove, or a pigeon because salvation is available to whosoever will place their faith in the shed blood of Jesus Christ regardless of their socio-economic status because "**... Of a truth ... God is no respecter of persons: But in every nation he that feareth him, and worketh righteousness, is accepted with him.**" (Acts 10:34-35).

This sacrifice was performed by the offeror bringing the substitute sin bearer to the alter and laying his hands on its head, thereby transferring his sin to the sin bearing sacrifice. He then slew it by cutting its throat, indicating that it was his sins that necessitated the death of the sacrifice. The blood was then drained and sprinkled around and upon the altar. Blood was sprinkled on the top, sides, and base of the alter indicating that there can be no access to God, from any direction, save through the shed blood of Jesus Christ. "**Jesus saith unto him, I am the way, the truth, and the life: no man cometh unto the Father, but by me.**" (Jn 14:6).

The whole animal was then meticulously dismembered and examined. After it was placed in an orderly fashion upon the alter, it was burnt to ashes, except for the hide, which was the offertory's portion. Examining the dismembered animal served to illustrate that Jesus Christ is our perfect sin-offering because " ... [He was] "**without sin**" (Heb 4:15) and "**... in him**

is no sin." (1 Jn 3:5). The complete consummation
of the sacrifice in the flames of the alter indicated that
the sinless Redeemer would face the full wrath of God
and be found totally acceptable to God because He "**...
knew no sin ...**" (2 Cor 5:21), and He "**... did no sin ...**"
(1 Pet 2:22). The hide was left for the offeror indicating
that God has no use for willful flesh and that the flesh
has no intrinsic life within itself, but is useful to man,
providing he knows how to make it conform to his will.
Likewise, salvation of a soul has no profit for the flesh.
**" It is the spirit that quickeneth; the flesh profiteth
nothing ..."** (Jn 6:63).

Sin Offering

Up until the completion of the Tabernacle,
every personal sacrifice presented to God had been
a burnt offering. After God agreed to dwell with
man, foreshadowing Christ's arrival and the Holy
Spirit indwelling each and every believer, Moses was
commanded to performed a sin-offering. This blood
offering was required to consecrate the brazen alter,
and to cleanse and ordain the priests so they could serve
God in the Tabernacle and enter into the Holy of Holies.
This offering was a public admission that sacerdotalism
is forbidden. It illustrated that the priests were sinners
too and not superior to anyone nor righteous in their
own right. It was by this offering that the priests were
consecrated to God prior to being allowed to execute
their priestly duties.

To accomplish the sin-offering Aaron and his sons
placed their hands upon the head of the bullock offering
thereby fully identifying with it, and symbolically

transferring their sin to the sacrifice that was appointed to bear it. Similarly by faith, the sinner trusts in Jesus to bear his sin. Moses then slew the bullock. After the transfer of sin, death was immediately inflicted upon the appointed sacrifice, and so it was with Christ's death upon the cross.

Some of the shed blood was applied to the horns of the brazen alter, thereby acknowledging the righteous judgement of God for sin and the power of the blood to atone for sin. The horns of the alter represented the power or strength of the alter to remove sin.

The alter was constructed of what we call today Naval Brass (C46400). Naval Brass is a high strength, corrosion resistant and very hard material which ideally represents God's sovereign, incorruptible, and inflexible governance.

The remainder of the blood was poured on the ground at the base of the alter thereby establishing that remission of sin is only through the shed blood of the sin-offering. This blood also joined the blood of the righteous slain signifying that God would in the fullness of time shed the blood of the unrighteous in answer to the prayers of the saints; **"... saying, How long, O Lord, holy and true, dost thou not judge and avenge our blood on them that dwell on the earth?"** (Rev 6:10).

Likewise Jesus, the innocent substitute sacrifice for sinful man, (i.e. sin-offering) shed His blood on the alter, (i.e. the cross), thereby providing remission of sin for whosoever believeth in Him; **"And he [Jesus] took the cup, and gave thanks, and gave** *it* **to them, [his disciples] saying, Drink ye all of it; For this is my**

blood of the new covenant, which is shed for many for the remission of sins." (Matt 26:27-28) and **"... This cup *is* the new testament in my blood, which is shed for you."** (Lk 22:20).

The bullock's fat, caul above the liver, two kidneys and their associated fat was burnt upon the brazen alter. In the nostrils of God, these produced a sweet savour. Fat illustrated acknowledgement that all our prosperity, health and vigor is of God. The caul, or diaphragm (the mechanism whereby we draw every precious breath) illustrated acknowledgement that each and every breath of life is a gift of God, and that man cannot and did not will himself into existence nor can he **"... taking thought can add to his stature one cubit ..."** (Lk 12:25). The kidneys, (the organs that cleanse our blood) served as a confession that only God can cleanse us of sin. Our capacity for self-righteousness, our capability to cleanse ourselves of sin admittedly, are completely non-existent.

The remainder of the bullock was burnt to ashes outside the camp in a fierce consuming fire reminding man that God is a consuming fire, and the fires of Hell await all who trust in the flesh. The burnt head and brains, reminded all that **" ... the foolishness of God is wiser than men;..."** (1 Cor 1:25) and the burnt horns, bone and muscle tissue that **"... the weakness of God is stronger than men"** (1 Cor 1:25). The horns, hide and hair produced a horrific, nauseating, and unforgettable stench, alerting all to the fact that in the flesh dwelleth no good thing and sin is a stench in the nostrils of God.

It is interesting to note that the first time a person gets a whiff of burning flesh it creates uncontrollable nausea. However, upon each subsequent exposure ones reaction continually lessens until the smell becomes completely unnoticeable. And so it is with sin. Willfully committing sin for the first time produces a severely guilty conscience as a direct response to the violation to God's civil code; "**... when the Gentiles, which have not the law, do by nature the things contained in the law, these, having not the law, are a law unto themselves: [one's conscience] Which shew the work of the law written in their hearts, their conscience also bearing witness, ...**" (Rom 2:14-15). However, with each repetition, the guilt lessens until it evokes no reaction at all. At this juncture, the sin has lost its sinfulness and is considered as nothing less than normal. Sadly to say, at this point, those that would dare to label the sin as sin are resented and called prudes. Such is the subtle and deceptive nature of sin and its consequent downward spiral to Hell.

Immortality

The true value of immortality cannot be fully comprehended by time-constrained man. Because the life is in the blood, and therefore a symbol of the value of life we can only get an inkling of its true worth. The Passover is one of the Israelites most revered celebrations that wonderfully illustrates the value of Christ's blood; "**... Thus saith the Lord, About midnight will I go out into the midst of Egypt: And all the firstborn in the land of Egypt shall die, from the firstborn of Pharaoh that sitteth upon his throne, even unto the firstborn of the maidservant that *is* behind the mill: and all the firstborn of beasts. And there shall be a** great cry throughout all the land of Egypt, such as there was none like it, nor shall be like it anymore. But against any of the children of Israel shall not a dog move his tongue against man or beast, that ye may know how that the Lord doth put a difference between the Egyptians and Israel." (Ex 11:4-7).

God chose His words very carefully; He said that all the firstborn <u>of</u> (not <u>in</u>) the land of Egypt shall die. So while God condemned all in the land of Egypt, both Egyptians and Israelites alike, God also put a difference between the Egyptians and the Israelites. This difference did not result from anything the Israelites did or could do for themselves, it was the strictly by the grace of God that this difference was established. Those that did not die were saved from death by their faith in the saving blood of God's only begotten Son, Jesus Christ.

God told Moses to speak these words "**... unto all the congregation of Israel, saying, In the tenth *day* of this month they shall take to them every man a lamb, according to the house of *their* fathers, a lamb for an house ... Your lamb shall be without blemish, a male of the first year: ye shall take *it* out from the sheep, or from the goats: and ye shall keep it up until the fourteenth day of the same month: and the whole assembly of the congregation of Israel shall kill it in the evening. And they shall take of the blood, and strike *it* on the two side posts and on the upper door post of the houses, wherein they shall eat it. ... And thus shall ye eat it; *with* your loins girded, your shoes on your feet, and your staff in your hand; and ye shall eat it in haste: it *is* the LORD'S Passover. For I will pass through the land of Egypt this night, and**

will smite all the firstborn in the land of Egypt, both man and beast: and against all the gods of Egypt I will execute judgment: I *am* the LORD. (Ex 12:3-12).

The death of the firstborn was a direct consequence of their sin, because death is the wages of sin. However, both the Egyptians and the Israelites were sinful in nature and in practice for **"... there is no difference [between any men]: For all have sinned and come short of the glory of God."** (Rom 3:22-23).

The good news is, God in His infinite mercy said, **"... where sin abounded, grace did much more abound."** (Rom 5:20). God provided a substitute. The sentence of death was executed against all of the land, however for those who had faith in the blood, it fell upon an innocent victim. The only deciding and saving factor between life and death was not personal character, genetic superiority, or religious zeal, it was based solely on one's faith in the blood of the Lord's Passover Lamb. It was in the blood of the Lamb where **"Mercy and truth met together and righteousness and peace kissed *each other.*"** (Psm 85:10).

King David fully understood the value of fellowship with God, the value of salvation, the value of eternal life, and the value of Christ's blood better than we are able to today. He expressed this value the only way it could demonstrated, through the shed blood of valuable livestock. The very best livestock and the only means they had of making a living, by the sweat of their face, on this cursed earth were sacrificed; **"... So David went and brought up the ark of God from the house of Obededom into the city of David with gladness. And it was so, that when they that bare the ark of the**

LORD had gone six paces, he sacrificed oxen and fatlings. And David danced before the LORD with all *his* might; and David *was* girded with a linen ephod. So David and all the house of Israel brought up the ark of the LORD with shouting and with the sound of the trumpet." (2 Sam 6:12-15).

Just to get a rough approximation of how much blood was shed a top-level analysis is presented;

Assumptions
- King David's journeyed from the house of Obededom into the city of David
- King David's majestic procession moves at approximately the same rate that the Roman army traveled = 10 miles per 12 hour day
- No mention is made of an encampment en route so journey made in 1 day= 10 miles
- 2 bulls and 2 sheep sacrificed per sacrifice

Calculations
- The volume of blood in milliliters of sheep and cattle is approximately 6% of the body weight in grams
- Grams = Pounds X 453.6 grams/pound
- 6% X weight of animal in grams = milliliters of blood
- milliliters of blood X .0003 gallons/milliliter = gallons of blood
- Oxen weigh between 397 – 2,425 lbs. Nominal weight- 1,433 lbs.
- 1,433 lb ox = 12 gallons of blood per ox
- Sheep weigh between 88 - 265 lbs. Nominal

weight- 141 lbs.
- 141 lb sheep = 1.2 gallons of blood per sheep
- Total gallons of blood per sacrifice = 26.4 gallons
- 1 pace = 2 ½ feet
- Sacrifice every 6 paces = 15 feet
- 10 mile journey = 52,800 feet
- 52,800 foot journey with sacrifices every 15 feet = 3,520 sacrifices
- 3,520 sacrifices X 26.4 gallons of blood per sacrifice

Results
- 14,080 animals were sacrificed
- Every 15 feet 26 gallons of blood was poured onto the ground in front of the men carrying the ark
- The arc was carried to Jerusalem over ground that was literally awash in blood

Considering that each animal sacrificed had to be the best livestock available and all without blemish one can start to grasp the true value of the blood Christ shed on our behalf. King David rejoiced for it; **"... David danced before the LORD with all *his* might ..."** in the midst of the gallons and gallons of blood that were poured out on the ground.

Likewise David's son, King Solomon, also highly valued the blood. He too demonstrated his appreciation for the blood that Christ was to shed; **"Thus all the work that Solomon made for the house of the LORD was finished: and Solomon brought in *all* the things that David his father had dedicated; and the silver, and the gold, and all the instruments, put he among** the treasures of the house of God. Then Solomon assembled the elders of Israel, and all the heads of the tribes, the chief of the fathers of the children of Israel, unto Jerusalem, to bring up the ark of the covenant of the LORD out of the city of David, which *is* Zion. Wherefore all the men of Israel assembled themselves unto the king in the feast which *was* in the seventh month. And all the elders of Israel came; and the Levites took up the ark. And they brought up the ark, and the tabernacle of the congregation, and all the holy vessels that *were* in the tabernacle, these did the priests *and* the Levites bring up. Also king Solomon, and all the congregation of Israel that were assembled unto him before the ark, sacrificed sheep and oxen, which could not be told nor numbered for multitude. And the priests brought in the ark of the covenant of the LORD unto his place, to the oracle of the house, into the most holy *place, even* under the wings of the cherubims:" (2 Chron 5:1-7).

Just to get a rough approximation of how much blood was shed a top-level analysis is presented;

Assumptions

- 10,000 is the number used in scripture indicate innumerable, without number, or an infinite number
- Total number of oxen sacrificed = 10,000 = 120,000 gallons of blood
- Total number of sheep sacrificed = 10,000 = 12,000 gallons of blood
- Total gallons of blood shed = 132,000 gallons
- King Solomon's journey to bring up the ark of the

covenant of the LORD out of the city of David to
the Temple = 2.5 mile
- 1 pace = 2 ½ feet
- Sacrifice performed every 6 paces
- 6 paces = 15 feet
- 2 ½ mile journey = 13,200 feet

Calculations
- 13,200 foot journey with sacrifices every 15 feet = 880 sacrifices
- 132,000 total gallons of blood / 880 sacrifices = 150 gallons of blood per sacrifice

Results
- 20,000 animals were sacrificed
- Every 15 feet 150 gallons of blood was poured on the ground in front of the men carrying the ark
- The arc was carried to the temple through a literal river of blood

After King Solomon had completed the temple he dedicated it with a national, fourteen day, sacrifice and feast to show appreciation for the goodness and mercy God had shown to Israel and in appreciation of the blood atonement that Christ would make; **"And Solomon offered a sacrifice of peace offerings, which he offered unto the LORD, two and twenty thousand oxen, and an hundred and twenty thousand sheep. So the king and all the children of Israel dedicated the house of the LORD."** (1 Kings 6:63). **"And at that time Solomon held a feast, and all Israel with hem, a great congregation, from the entering in of**

**Hamath unto the river of Egypt, before the LORD
our God, seven days and seven days, even fourteen
days. On the eighth day he sent the people away:
and the blessed the king, and went unto their tents
joyful and glad of heart for all the goodness that the
LORD had done for David his servant, and for Israel
his people."** (1 Kings 8:65-66).

Just to get a rough approximation of how much
blood was shed a top-level analysis is presented;

Assumptions
- Total number of oxen sacrificed = 22,000 =
  264,000 gallons of blood
- Total number of sheep sacrificed = 120,000 =
  144,000 gallons of blood
- Feast lasted 14 days
- Sacrifices performed 10 hours per day

Results
- 142,000 animals were sacrificed
- 408,000 gallons of blood were shed during the 14
  day feast
- 2,914 gallons of blood were shed every hour for
  14 days
- The brazen alter stood in the midst of a literal lake
  of blood

Holy Blood

Conception by the Holy Ghost was the only way
the virgin birth could have been accomplished. Jesus
was the promised seed of the woman spoken of in
Genesis. Mary provided the means whereby Jesus was

born, according to the flesh. His birthright and claim
to David's Kingdom came through his male caretaker,
Joseph. However, it was the Holy Spirit that provided
the needed male element for Mary's conception and
Jesus' blood. Because, Jesus' blood did not come from
Joseph it was absolutely sinless blood. It was divine
blood. It was Holy blood and there has never been nor
ever will be any other like it.

Jesus was conceived free of Adam's sin. **"Now
the birth of Jesus Christ was on this wise: When as
his mother Mary was espoused to Joseph, before
they came together, she was found with child of the
Holy Ghost. Then Joseph her husband, being a just
man, and not willing to make her a public example,
was minded to put her away privily. But while he
thought on these things, behold, the angel of the
Lord appeared unto him in a dream, saying, Joseph,
thou son of David, fear not to take unto thee Mary
thy wife: for that which is conceived in her is of the
Holy Ghost. And she shall bring forth a son, and
thou shalt call his name JESUS: for he shall save his
people from their sins. Now all this was done, that it
might be fulfilled which was spoken of the Lord by
the prophet, saying, Behold, a virgin shall be with
child, and shall bring forth a son, and they shall call
his name Emmanuel, which being interpreted is,
God with us. Then Joseph being raised from sleep
did as the angel of the Lord had bidden him, and
took unto him his wife: And knew her not till she
had brought forth her firstborn son: and he called
his name JESUS."** (Matt 1:18-25).

Luke the physician, who had perfect understanding

of all things from the very first, receiving the facts from eyewitnesses, and ministers of the Word also recounts the story of Jesus' immaculate conception; **"And in the sixth month the angel Gabriel was sent from god unto a city of Galilee, named Nazareth, To a virgin espoused to a man whose name was Joseph, of the house of David; and the virgin's name *was* Mary. And the angel came in unto her, and said, Hail, *thou that art* highly favoured, the Lord *is* with thee: blessed *art* thou among women. And when she saw *him*, she was troubled at his saying, and cast in her mind what manner of salutation this should be. And the angel said unto her, Fear not, Mary: for thou hast found favour with God. And, behold, thou shalt conceive in thy womb, and bring forth a son, and shalt call his name JESUS. He shall be great, and shall be called the son of the Highest: and the Lord God shall give unto him the throne of his father David: And he shall reign over the house of Jacob for ever; and of his kingdom there shall be no end. Then said Mary unto the angel, How shall this be, seeing I know not a man? And the angel answered and said unto her, The Holy ghost shall come upon thee, and the power of the Highest shall overshadow thee: therefore also that holy thing which shall be born of thee shall be called the Son of God."** (Lk 1:26-35).

Our Lord was innocent of the charge of being a sinner. This was confirmed by Judas Iscariot himself when he confessed; **"... I have betrayed the innocent blood..."** (Mat 27:4). Jesus came like unto us in the *likeness* of sinful flesh.

Impeccable

Jesus was impeccable, that is incapable of sinning, free from any fault or blame. His blood was pure sinless blood because His father was God. It is because His blood was not contaminated with the sin of Adam and consequently He was the only one qualified to "**... taste death for every man.**" (Heb 2:9). And because Jesus "**humbled himself and became obedient unto death, even the death of the cross. Wherefore God also hath highly exalted him, and given him a name which is above every name: That at the name of Jesus every knee should bow, of *things* in heaven [all the saints, all the angels, all the Cherubims, and all the Seraphims] and *things* in earth [every man, woman, and child] and *things* under the earth [every demon, every lost soul in Hell, and Satan himself]; And that every tongue should confess that Jesus Christ is Lord, to the glory of God the Father.**" (Phil 2:8-9).

Bloody Birth

After the wise men from the East worshipped Jesus and presented their gifts of gold, and frankincense, and myrrh to Him they departed into their own country another way without returning to Herod. "**Then Herod, when he saw that he was mocked of the wise men, was exceeding wroth, and sent forth, and slew all the children that were in Bethlehem, and in all the coasts thereof, from two years old and under, according to the time which he had diligently enquired of the wise men. Then was fulfilled that which was spoken by Jeremy the prophet, saying, In Rama was there**

a voice heard, lamentation, and weeping, and great mourning, Rachel weeping for her children, and would not be comforted, because they are not." (Matt 2:16-18).

History has proven that, then as now, citizens have more to fear from their own Governments than they do from attacking countries. Herod shed the blood of his own innocent subjects in an attempt to maintain his worldly power. Since Herod's days this same ruthless quest for power has taken the lives of millions of innocent people. The blood of those that were saved, still cry out to God for justice, even to this day. It is reassuring to know that we can be absolutely sure that justice will be served for God said, **"...Vengeance is mine, I will repay..."** (Rom 12:19). And not only will justice be served but it will be served sooner than most unthinking people realize, for the King **is** coming. The King is coming back to set up His kingdom and to judge the quick and the dead.

It is interesting to note that this mass execution by a people's own Government was not a new phenomenon. Haman had plans to slaughter every Jew between India and Ethiopia. **"And the letters were sent by posts into all the king's provinces, to destroy, to kill, and to cause to perish, all Jews, both young and old, little children and women, in one day, *even* upon the thirteenth *day* of the twelfth month, which is the month Adar, and *to take* the spoil of them for a prey."** (Esther 3:13).

Pharaoh ordered the merciless killing of every newborn male Hebrew child as part of Satan's attempt to prevent the promised Messiah from coming; **"And** the king of Egypt spake to the Hebrew midwives, of which the name of the one *was* Shiphrah, and the name of the other Puah: And he said, When ye do the office of a midwife to the Hebrew women, and see *them* upon the stools; if it *be* a son, then ye shall kill him: but if it *be* a daughter, then she shall live." (Ex 1:15-16).

Sad to say, this practice of selected extermination has not ceased. It is estimated that prior to 1900 over 133 million people have been murdered by their own Governments, and from the years 1900-1999, approximately 174 million people have been murdered by their own Governments. The only conclusion that can be drawn is that the Bible is correct, man is getting worse not better. Statistics support the sobering fact that one is more likely to be murdered by one's own Government than to die in war against another country and leads one to the conclusion that the more totalitarian the government the more likely mass execution of its citizens will be. Or said another way, the greater the control government has over the personal lives of its citizens the less it values those very same lives. Hence the old adage; absolute power corrupts absolutely. It will only be under the reign of King Jesus that this trend be reversed.

Bloody Garden

"And he [Jesus] was withdrawn from them about a stone's cast, and kneeled down, and prayed, Saying, Father, if thou be willing, remove this cup from me: nevertheless not my will, but thine, be done. And there appeared an angel unto him from

heaven, strengthening him. And being in an agony he prayed more earnestly: and his sweat was as it were great drops of blood falling down to the ground." (Lk 22:41-44).

Some may say that Christ's sweating blood is nothing more than a figure of speech, however, the Bible says what is means and means what it says. Jesus did in fact sweat blood. The problem before Christians today is that they are **"... rich, and increased with goods, and have need of nothing; and knowest not that thou art wretched, and miserable, and poor, and blind, and naked."** (Rev 3:17).

Many Christians, I am sure, desire to have such a close and earnest relationship with the Lord that they could sweat blood during prayer; however, by the same token who today could truly realize or want to experience the necessary sufferings that would accompany such a capability?

Most modern Christians, in this Laodician Age, do not fully realize that even through their best efforts, they will only squeeze through the gates of Glory by **"... the skin of their teeth."** (Job 19:20). While our pharmaceutical industry has been a great blessing and contributed to our physical comforts, it on the other hand has deprived us of the warning of the reality of Hell that people who die in their sins provide. In the modern drugged demise of people today who can note the marked difference between a Christian's death and a heathens? It is reported that King Charles of France feared his impending death so greatly that he literally sweated blood. King Charles (responsible for the persecution of the French Huguenots) realized too late that **"the eyes of the LORD *are* in every place, beholding the evil and the good"** (Prov. 15:3) and that **"... God is angry with the wicked every day."** (Psm 7:11). He realized too late **"It *is* a fearful thing to fall into the hands of the living God."** (Heb 10:31) and that he was soon to stand before a thrice Holy God and give an account for the brutal death of God's children.

Additionally, some say that Jesus was afraid of the forthcoming scourging and crucifixion and this is the reason He sweated blood. This is definitely not the reason. Jesus looked forward to His death on the cross as a necessity. Jesus sweated blood while in earnest prayer because He knew that He was going to have to face the full, unabated wrath of His Father as payment for our sins. The Son of God knew only too well the extent and magnitude of His Fathers fiery indignation. Jesus had seen the full unabated wrath of the Lord and this is the reason why Jesus prayed for another method of sin payment. Remember, Jesus was with the Father and witnessed first-hand His fury when He annihilated everyone on earth via the worldwide flood and He also witnessed His fierce rage as He totally obliterated Sodom and Gomorrah from off the face of the earth. Consequently, it is no wonder that Jesus Himself warned, **"...I will forewarn you whom ye shall fear: Fear him, which after he hath killed hath power to cast into hell; yea, I say unto you Fear him."** (Lk 12:5) because **"It *is* a fearful thing to fall into the hands of the living God."** (Heb 10:31).

Therefore, if Jesus' fear of the wrath of God drove Him to such earnest prayer that He sweated blood how much more should we **"... work out [our] own** salvation with fear and trembling[?]" (Phil 2:12).

Shedding Of Christ's Blood

"Pilate therefore, willing to release Jesus, spake again to them. But they cried, saying, Crucify *him*, crucify him. And he said unto them the third time, Why, what evil hath he done? I have found no cause of death in him: I will therefore chastise him, and let *him* go. And they were instant with loud voices, requiring that he might be crucified. And the voices of them and of the chief priests prevailed. And Pilate gave sentence that it should be as they required. And he released unto them him that for sedition and murder was cast into prison, whom they had desired; but he delivered Jesus to their will. And as they led him away, they laid hold upon one Simon, a Cyrenian, coming out of the country, and on him they laid the cross, that he might bear *it* after Jesus." (Lk 23:20-26).

"And when they were come to the place, which is called Calvary, there they crucified him, and the malefactors, one on the right hand, and the other on the left." (Lk 23:33). "And the people stood beholding. And the rulers also with them derided *him*, saying, He saved others; let him save himself, if he be Christ, the chosen of God. And the soldiers also mocked him, coming to him, and offering him vinegar, And saying, If thou be the king of the Jews, save thyself." (Lk 23:35-37).

"And it was about the sixth hour, and there was a darkness over all the earth until the ninth hour. And the sun was darkened, and the veil of the temple

was rent in the midst. And when Jesus had cried with a loud voice, he said, Father, into thy hands I commend my spirit: and having said thus, he gave up the ghost. Now when the centurion saw what was done, he glorified God, saying, Certainly this was a righteous man." (Lk 23:44-47).

Christ shed His blood **"… which taketh away the sin of the world."** (Jn 1:29). Jesus allowed himself to be brought before civilian and religious government. There He was convicted of claiming to be God (not of sin) and was sentenced to death, the death of the cross. Like a lamb that doesn't make a sound while being sheared, Jesus too never flinched, cried out in pain nor even so much as uttered a sound during His subsequent scourging, mocking, journey to Calvary, and crucifixion where He **"… endured the cross, despising the shame…"** (Heb 12:2).

Bloody Scourging

The Roman execution process was severe and designed to deter all others from ever committing a similar crime; **"When Pilate saw that he could prevail nothing, but *that* rather a tumult was made, he took water, and washed *his* hands before the multitude, saying, I am innocent of the blood of this just person: see ye *to it*. Then answered all the people, and said, His blood *be* on us, and on our children, Then released he Barabbas unto them: and when he had scourged Jesus, he delivered *him* to be crucified."** (Matt 27:24-26).

Scourging was the legal preliminary to every Roman execution. Only women, Roman senators, and Roman soldiers were ever exempted. The scourge was a short whip formed of three lashes, each made of leather or small cords with lead balls and iron sharps attached to the ends of each lash. The scourge, sometimes referred to as a scorpion, was designed to debilitate and inflict excruciating pain. A scorpion is what King Rehoboam threatened to scourge his populous within 2 Chronicles 10:11 when the said, **"… my father chastised you with whips, but I *will chastise you* with scorpions"**.

The Levitical Law dictated that no more than 40 lashes could be administered to a victim at any one time. **"And it shall be, if the wicked man be worthy to be beaten, that the judge shall cause him to lie down, and to be beaten before his face, according to his fault, by a certain number. Forty stripes he may give him, and not exceed: lest, *if* he should exceed, and beat him above these with many stripes, then thy brother should seem vile unto thee."** (Deut 25:2-3). Historians say that scourging devastates the body so severely, that if one were to receive more than 40 stripes the victim would most likely die as a result. Consequently, the victim was given a maximum of thirteen strokes with the scourge resulting in thirty-nine stripes being administered.

For scourging, the man was stripped of his clothing, and tied face down over a large stone or a low wooden structure. The back was flogged either by two soldiers or by one who alternated positions. The severity of the scourging depended on the disposition of the soldier(s) which weaken and debilitated the victim to a state just short of physical collapse.

As the Roman soldiers struck the victim's back, the

leather thongs with their attached lead balls and iron sharps, caused deep contusions and cut into the victim's subcutaneous tissues. As the scourging continued, the lacerations would tear into the underlying skeletal muscles and produce literal rivulets of blood. It is the extent of blood loss that usually determined how long the victim would survive on the cross.

One of the effects of scourging is pleurisy. Pleurisy is the inflammation and swelling of the pleura. The visceral pleura is a thin lining that covers the lungs and the parietal pleura lines the inside of the rib cage. The tiny intervening space between these two linings is called the pleural cavity. Normally there is only 3 to 4 teaspoons of fluid in the pleural cavity. The fluid acts as a lubricant allowing the two pleural linings to slide over each other during respiration. In severe cases of pleurisy, excess fluid seeps into the pleural cavity, resulting in pleural effusion.

Pleurisy can be caused by other conditions besides trauma to the rib cage (i.e. scourging). Some of the common causes for pleurisy include, pneumonia, viral infection of the lower respiratory system, tuberculosis, rheumatoid arthritis, lupus, pulmonary embolism, liver disease, pancreatitis and cancer.

As a direct result of the scourging Jesus developed pleural effusion. This can be deduced by the knowledge that Jesus was our sacrifice and was **"... as of a lamb without blemish and without spot"** (1 Pet 1:19), hence all infectious and illness related causes of pleural effusion can be ruled out.

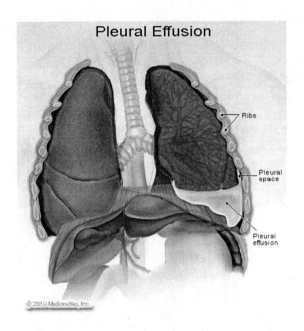

The fact that Jesus faced the scourging head-on is attested to in Isaiah 50:5-6; **"The Lord GOD hath opened mine [Jesus'] ear, and I [Jesus] was not rebellious, neither turned away back. I [Jesus] gave my back to the smiters, …"**

We also know that the scourging was extremely brutal and would certainly cause pleural effusion because Psalms 129:3 states; **"The plowers plowed upon my back: they made long their furrows."** And while the Levitical Law is very clear that **"Forty stripes he may give him, *and* not exceed"** (Deut 25:3), Jesus was scourged far beyond this limit because he was; **"… delivered into the hands of sinful men …"** (Lk 24:7) and **"… Pilate gave sentence that it should be as they [the chief priests] required."** (Lk 23:24). As a result of the severe scourging; **"... many were astonied at thee [Jesus]; his visage was so marred more than any man, and his form more than the sons of men."** (Isa 52:14).

The Apostle Paul was scourged five times with thirty nine stripes each; **"Of the Jews five times received I forty *stripes* save one"** (2 Cor. 11:24) yet no mention is made of his visage being marred. Consequently, it can be concluded that Jesus, because of His perceived blasphemy by declaring Himself equal with God, was scourged above and beyond that which was prescribed by the Levitical Law. He was truly delivered into the hands of sinful men.

God however maketh all things work together for good that love him. For even though; **"... the LORD hath laid on him the iniquity of us all;"** (Isa 53:6) **"... he *was* wounded for our transgressions, *he was* bruised for our iniquities: the chastisement of our peace *was* upon him; and with his stripes we are healed."** (Isa 53:5).

Throughout the entire scourging Jesus did not writhe, flinch, murmur or let out one cry for we are told that; **"He was oppressed, and he was afflicted, yet he opened not his mouth: he is brought as a lamb to the slaughter, and as a sheep before her shearers is dumb, so he openeth not his mouth. "** (Isa 53:7). This superhuman ability to remain still and silent resulted in an illegal number of stripes (more than 40) as His silence surely must have infuriated the High Priests and scribes. It was because thirty-nine stripes failed to make Him cry out even once that it can be concluded that the beating continued until the Roman soldiers either tired or became embarrassed realizing that they were incapable of scourging Jesus severely enough to make Him cry out. Either way, they eventually ceased the scourging and led Him away. It is a certainty that the centurion took notice that Jesus was an exceptional person, for it was quite out of the norm for any man to have survived such a harsh scourging.

Bloody Hall

Blood was shed here too for the Bible informs us that the Roman soldiers not only tore out his beard; **"I gave my back to the smiters, and my cheeks to them that plucked off the hair: I hid not my face from shame and spitting."** (Isa 50:6) but they also beat a crown of thorns down onto his brow with a stout reed; **"... and when he had scourged Jesus, he delivered *him* to be crucified. Then the soldiers of the governor took Jesus into the common hall, and gathered unto him the whole band *of soldiers*. And they stripped him, and put on him a scarlet robe. And when they had platted a crown of thorns, they put it upon his head, and a reed in his right hand: and they bowed the knee before him, and mocked him, saying, Hail, King of the Jews! And they spit upon him, and took the reed, and smote him on the head. And after that they had mocked him, they took the robe off from him, and put his own raiment on him, and let him away to crucify *him*."** (Matt 27:26-31).

By being crowned with the bloody crown of thorns, driven down through His scalp and forehead, and wearing it during His crucifixion, Christ lifted God's curse off the earth; **"... cursed *is* the ground for thy** sake; in sorrow shalt thou eat *of* it all the days of thy life; Thorns also and thistles shall it bring forth to thee; and thou shalt eat the herb of the field;"(Gen 3:17-18).

It is because Jesus took away the curse of the world that we can look forward to Millennial Kingdom where; **"... the plowman shall overtake the reaper, and the treader of grapes him that soweth seed; and the mountains shall drop sweet wine, and all the hills shall melt."** (Amos 9:13) and **"The wolf also shall dwell with the lamb, and the leopard shall lie down with the kid; and the calf and the young lion and the fatling together; and a little child shall lead them. And the cow and the bear shall feed; their young ones shall lie down together: and the lion shall eat straw like the ox. And the sucking child shall play on the hole of the asp, and the weaned child shall put his hand on the cockatrice's den. They shall not hurt nor destroy in all my holy mountain: for the earth shall be full of the knowledge of the LORD, as the waters cover the sea."** (Isa 11:6-9).

Bloody Road To Mount Calvary

After the scourging and the heretical mocking, Jesus was led out of the Praetorium and; **"... many were astonied at thee [Jesus]; his visage was so marred more than any man, and his form more than the sons of men."** (Isa 52:14). Never-the-less Jesus set His face like a flint, shouldered the cross He was destined to be crucified on and headed towards Mount Calvary; **"... And they took Jesus, and led him away. And he bearing his cross went forth into a place called *the***

place of a skull, which is called in Hebrew Golgotha:
Where they crucified him, and two other with him,
on either side one, and Jesus in the midst." (Jn 19:14-
18). "And as they led him away, they laid hold upon
one Simon, a Cyrenian, coming out of the country,
and on him they laid the cross, that he might bear *it*
after Jesus." (Lk 24:20-26).

Jesus was not rebellious, neither turned away or
back but set His face like a flint, and worked His will
upon His flesh. He stooped down, shouldered His cross
and set out without hesitation towards Mount Calvary to
accomplish His divine mission.

The average weight of a Roman cross was
approximately, 300 pounds. History informs us that it
was customary for the condemned man to shoulder his
own cross from the scourging site to the site of crucifixion
outside the city walls. Sometimes, due to the severity
of the scourging the condemned was so weakened that
he was only able to bear the cross' horizontal crossbar.
The crossbar weighed approximately 75 to 125 pounds
and was placed across the nape of the victim's neck and
balanced across his shoulders. The convicted criminal's
arms were then outstretched and tied to the crossbar to
be sure he would not drop it.

From the words used in Scripture, one can be sure
that Jesus did indeed shoulder His crucifix and not just
the crossbar. This can logically be concluded because
the Bible clearly states that Simon was compelled to bear
his **cross**. Simon was an innocent bystander and not
convicted on any infraction of the law. Therefore, under
Roman Law Simon could not have had the crucifix's
cross member tied across his shoulders signifying that

he was a condemned criminal without due process first being served.

From a natural man's vantage, Simon was in the wrong place at the wrong time. In reality, Simon was actually in the right place at the right time. Because of Simon's faith, he had brought his family all the way from Cyrenaica to celebrate the Passover in Jerusalem. We know he was the spiritual leader of his home like Abraham because in Romans 16:13 the Apostle Paul salutes Simon's son, Rufus, as **"… chosen in the Lord …"**. Similar to the favor shown to the Virgin Mary, God showed favor to Simon by allowing him the privilege of bearing His Son's cross (alter of sacrifice) to Golgotha. Simon should also serve as an example for us all because he obeyed the commandments of Scripture which says **"And whosoever shall compel thee to go a mile, go with him twain."** (Matt 5:41) and **"… endure hardness as a good soldier of Jesus Christ."** (2 Tim 2:3). Blessings come in many different forms besides material gain.

It is important to note that there is no evidence anywhere in Scripture to support the commonly held belief that Jesus dropped his cross or was unable to bear it to Mount Calvary. The heretics that promulgate these myths deny the fact that Jesus was God made in the likeness of sinful flesh.

The centurion impressed Simon into Roman service out of embarrassment and mercy. The centurion was very familiar with executions by crucifixion, and it is certain that the uniqueness of these proceeding did not go unnoticed. The battle-hardened centurion was half embarrassed because he realized the impossibility for a mere mortal to have survived the most severe scourging his company was able to inflict on a person and the impossibility of such a scourged person to squat down, place a 300 pound crucifix upon his shoulder, and then unaided, stand erect and march down the road to his own execution. The feelings of mercy came from the centurion's heart being pricked by the Holy Ghost, just like Saul's was at the stoning of Stephen. The Lord continued to work on the heart of the centurion and his whole company were brought to repentance and their souls were saved from the damnation of Hell at the conclusion of the crucifixion; **"Now when the centurion, and they that were with him, watching Jesus, saw the earthquake, and those things that were done, they feared greatly, saying, Truly, this was the Son of God."** (Matt 27:54).

An important item to note from the above is that the centurion and his company were saved from the wrath of God because they repented, and their repentance was due solely to their fear of the LORD. The Bible clearly commands us to; **"… Fear him, which after he hath killed hath power to cast into hell; yea, I say unto you, Fear him."** (Lk 12:5) and fear means fear, not respect, not acknowledgement, not the nonsensical vogue term "reverential fear" or anything else that is short of a humbling, knee bowing, tear producing, mercy begging, fear that your soul is destined for the flames of Hell unless Jesus steps into your heart and saves your low down sinful soul. Remember, **"The fear of the LORD *is* a fountain of life, to depart from the snares of death."** (Prov 14:7).

There is a very common misconception in today's

Christendom that people can have their souls saved by just knowing that "God loves them". The meaning of **"… God so loved the world, that he gave his only begotten Son, …"** (Jn 3:16) is that God, so loved the world, that He made a provision for mankind to be saved from the damnation of Hell, and that provision is faith in Jesus Christ, God's only begotten Son. However for faith to be crystallized into a saving faith, vice just an acknowledgement and superficial belief, that Jesus is God's Son, requires repentance and only a true fear of the LORD and the fear of judgement to come, brings about such repentance. Unless you truly fear the Lord, knowing **"… the LORD thy God *is* a consuming fire, even a jealous God."** (Deut 4:24) and fully realize **"It *is* a fearful thing to fall into the hands of the living God"** (Heb 10:31), and admit to God in fear and trembling, with no reservations, that you have no righteousness of your own and are nothing but a worthless sinner and deserve being damned to Hell for sins committed against a thrice Holy God, and beg Jesus to save your soul from the flames of Hell, you haven't truly repented and hence your soul is still Hell bound. Remember and take to heart what Matthew Henry so wisely advised; *"We must not repent that we have repented, but we must repent that we have not repented better"*.

Bloody Crucifixion

Death by crucifixion was used primarily for slaves, rebels, pirates, enemies of the State and criminals. Consequently, crucifixion was considered the most shameful and disgraceful way a person could die. **"And they crucified him, and parted his garments, casting**

lots: that it might be fulfilled which was spoken by
the prophet, they parted my garments among them,
and upon my vesture did they cast lots. And sitting
down they watched him there; And set up over his
head his accusation written, THIS IS JESUS THE
KING OF THE JEWS." (Matt 27:35-37). "Now
from the sixth hour there was darkness over all the
land unto the ninth hour. And about the ninth hour
Jesus cried with a loud voice, saying, Eli, Eli, lama
sabachthani? that is to say, My God, my God, why
hast thou forsaken me?" (Matt 27:45-46). "Jesus,
when he had cried again with a loud voice, yielded
up the ghost." (Matt 27:50).

The Romans had a standard procedure for crucifying
the condemned. The crucifix was laid on the ground
and the condemned was laid on his back on top of it.
The arms were outstretched and 3/8 inch square nails,
approximately 6 inches long, were driven between
the two bones of the forearm (the radius and the ulna)
just above the wrist. Next, the knees were bent until
the feet were flat on the crucifix vertical. Once in this
position, one foot was placed on atop the other a single
nail driven through both feet (through the first or second
intermetatarsal space, just distal to the tarsometatarsal
joint). Once the condemned man was secured to the
crucifix, it was up-righted and dropped in a hole that had
previously been dug for it.

A person crucified in this manner was for all
practical purposes locked onto the cross. With a person
nailed in position and the cross uprighted, the weight
of the body, pulling down on the forearms forced the
nails up into the "V" shaped space formed by the head

of the ulna and the radius. The sides of the square nails dug into the bones thereby locking the person onto the cross. Escape was an impossibility. The more a person struggled the more securely held they became. In fact, a person crucified in this manner would stay on the crucifix long after the birds of prey had picked their bones clean.

The goal of Roman crucifixion was not just to kill the criminal, but to maximize the malefactor's suffering as well as dishonor their body as a public reminder to anyone who might be thinking of violating Roman Law. The major physiologic effect of crucifixion, besides the excruciating pain, was a marked interference with normal respiration, particularly exhalation. The weight of the body, pulling down on the outstretched arms and shoulders, would tend to fix the intercostals muscles in an inhalation state and thereby hinder passive exhalation. Accordingly, exhalation was primarily diaphragmatic, and breathing was shallow. This type of shallow respiration does not provide sufficient oxygenation of the blood and carbon dioxide build-up in the blood (hypercarbia) results. The onset of muscle cramps (titanic contractions), due to fatigue and hypercarbia, hinder respiration even further.

To adequately exhale the victim was required to lift his body up by pushing down on the nailed feet and flexing the elbows and adducting the shoulders. This breathing process places the entire weight of the body on the feet and causes excruciating pain. Flexion of the elbows rotates the two bones of the forearm (the radius and the ulna) just above the wrist about the iron nails and causes severe pain via the median nerves. Lifting of the body for exhalation also scrapes the scourged back against the rough wooden vertical post. Consequently, each respiration becomes an agonizing and tiring ordeal that eventually led to death by asphyxiation. Muscle cramps of the outstretched and uplifted arms add the final touches to one of the most slow and agonizing deaths ever concocted by the mind of sinful man.

Some try to rationalize the impossibility of a body hanging on a crucifix by nails driven through the hands by saying that the Bible's use of the word *hand* really means, *wrists*. They claim nails were driven between the radius and the carpals or between the two rows of carpal bones, either proximal to or through the strong band like flexor retinaculum and the various intercarpal ligaments.

Genesis 24:22, 30 and 47, where Rebekah had bracelets **upon** *her hands,* are quoted to justify this hypothesis. The argument goes like this; bracelets are worn on the wrist, not on the hand. Because the word *upon* means *resting or being on the top of* or *on the surface of*, therefore, *hand* really means *wrist*. This line of logic is flawed, because the correct meaning for *upon* used in this instance means, *near to* and consequently *hand* does truly indeed mean *hand*.

Improperly defining words in Scripture is the basis for many cults. Acts 2:38 is an excellent example. This verse is commonly quoted to justify baptismal regeneration by the inappropriate definition of the word "for". **"Then Peter said unto them, Repent, and be baptized every one of you in the name of Jesus Christ for the remission of sins, and ye shall receive the gift of the Holy Ghost."** Cults define *for* to mean- *in order*

to obtain: *towards the obtaining of ... or possession of.*
However the correct definition, and the one substantiated
throughout Scripture is really, *because; on account of* or
by reason of.

Wrist cannot be substituted for the word *hand* for
an anatomical reason too. A person crucified with nails
driven through the wrists would tear off the cross just
like someone nailed through the hands because there is
inadequate structure in the wrist to support the weight of
a human body. National Geographic Channel's *Quest
for Truth: the Crucifixion*, performed an experiment to
determine if a person could indeed remain on a cross if
nailed through the wrists. They determined it is only
possible for a person to be crucified with nails driven
through the space between the two rows of carpal bones
if the feet were nailed to the **sides** of the vertical post.
This way the body's weight is supported by the legs, and
thereby sufficiently reduces the strain on the wrist tissue
to allow a body to remain on the cross.

Neither Scripture nor historical records support this
method of crucifixion. Per Roman standard procedure,
Jesus' feet were nailed to the front of the vertical post,
one atop the other, by means of a single 3/8 inch square
iron spike. If this standard procedure had not been used,
it would have been noted in Scripture.

Another heretical theory abounds regarding the
crucifixion of Christ. This theory postulates that Christ
was actually tied to the cross' horizontal crossbar with
ropes, just below each elbow. The Romans then drove
nails through his hands just to be mean and to make the
crucifixion more painful. The proponents of this heresy
acknowledge that nails were driven through Christ's

hands but, because the tissue of the hand is structurally very weak, the Romans tied Jesus to the cross to accomplish the crucifixion. Needless to say, this theory is not supported by Scripture and is nothing more than pure nonsense.

It is an anatomical fact that a mortal man, nailed to the cross through the palms of his hands and with one foot nailed atop the other to the front of the vertical post, cannot remain on a crucifix. The reason for this is, there are no structures in the hand strong enough to support the weight of the body. What happens is, the nails just rip through the tissue of the hand and the body consequently falls off the cross. It is important to note the Christ was crucified with neither a footrest nor a sedile. (A sedile is small protruding dowel on the vertical post that served as a "seat" thereby offloading some of the body's weight from the nails.)

The Bible likens the Roman Empire to iron, and quite rightly so, because Rome ruled the world with an iron fist. They crucified rebels and criminals to show the public that violation of Roman law would not be tolerated. Public executions are a very effective way of maintaining law and order and they had standard way of doing it. Jesus' crucifixion was no different than any other Roman crucifixion of that day **except** that they nailed him to the cross through the palms of his hands instead of between the two bones of the forearm (the radius and the ulna) just above the wrist.

Scripture documents this exception to standard procedures because it provides significant proof of Christ's Deity. The Apostle John provides the specifics; **"But Thomas, one of the twelve, called Didymus, was** not with them when Jesus came. The other disciples therefore said unto him, We have seen the Lord. But he said unto them, Except I shall see in his hands the print of the nails, and put my finger into the print of the nails, and thrust my hand into his side, I will not believe. And after eight days again his disciples were within, and Thomas with them: *then* came Jesus, the doors being shut, and stood in the midst, and said, Peace *be* unto you. Then saith he to Thomas, Reach hither thy finger, and behold my hands; and reach hither thy hand, and thrust *it* into my side: and be not faithless, but believing." (Jn 20:24-27).

Jesus remained on the cross by working His will upon His flesh. He clinched His fists thereby grasping the head of the nails and clung to the cross. It was by His own power that He remained on the cross.

Along with the unscriptural scourging, the Jewish priests and scribes saw to it that Jesus was nailed to the cross through the palms of His hands. This is validated by the taunting that accompanied the crucifixion;" And they that passed by railed on him, wagging their heads, and saying, Ah, thou that destroyest the temple, and buildest *it* in three days, Save thyself, and come down from the cross. Likewise also the chief priests mocking said among themselves with the scribes, He saved others; himself he cannot save. Let Christ the King of Israel descend now from the cross, that we may see and believe. And they that were crucified with him reviled him." (Mk 15:29-32). "And the people stood beholding. And the rulers also with them derided *him*, saying, He saved others; let him save himself, if he be Christ, the chosen of

God. And the soldiers also mocked him, coming to him, and offering him vinegar, And saying, If thou be the king of the Jews, save thyself." (Lk 23:35-37).

The chief priests and scribes knew that the flesh of a mortal's hand could not support one's body weight. They fully expected Christ to tear loose from the cross. This method of attachment was Satan's final attempt to foil God's perfect plan of salvation for mankind by preventing Jesus from dying on the cross. The Bible states; **"And if a man have committed a sin worthy of death, and he be to be put to death, and thou hang him on a tree: His body shall not remain all night upon the tree, but thus halt in any wise bury him that day; (for he that is hanged is accursed of God)"** (Deut 21:22-23). It was imperative that Christ die on the cross because Christ had to become a curse in order for remove the curse from mankind and the only way this could be accomplished in full agreement with Scripture, was to die <u>on</u> the cross.

Satan's plan was for Jesus' hands to rip free from the nails. With feet still securely nailed to the cross, He would fall forward in a headfirst arc towards the ground. Impacting headfirst on the ground, His neck, or some other bone, would have broken thereby voiding the prophetical necessities of His sacrificial death; **"… A bone of him shall not be broken."** (Jn 19:36).

However, because Jesus was God incarnate, and because He had set His face like a flint to die on the cross He worked His will upon His flesh and stayed on the cross despising the shame. For those skeptics that say crucifixion in this manner was impossible, one should take into consideration the following;

1. Jesus was beaten as no other man has ever been beaten yet He never so much as flinched or cried out once.

2. Jesus shouldered a 300 pound cross and headed to Calvary after he was scourged.

3. Jesus was able to cry out with a LOUD voice just prior to death. It is almost impossible for a person dying of hypercarbia (asphyxiation) to so much as whisper much less speak audibly. In addition to this, Jesus suffered from pleural effusion which reduces lung capacity and creates shortness of breath. Jesus however, **"cried with a loud voice, he said Father, into thy hands I commend my spirit: and having said thus, he gave up the ghost."** (Lk 23:46).

4. Jesus was physically stronger than Samson; **"... And they called for Samson out of the prison house; and he made them sport: and they set him between the pillars. And Samson said unto the lad that held him by the and, Suffer me that I may feel the pillars that I may lean upon them. Now the house was full of men and women; and all the lords of the Philistines *were* there; and *there were* upon the roof about three thousand men and women, that beheld while Samson made sport. And Samson called unto the LORD, and said, O Lord God, remember me, I pray thee, and strengthen me, I pray thee, only this once, O God, that I may be at once avenged of the Philistines for my two eyes. And Samson took hold of the two middle pillars upon which the house stood, and on which it**

was borne up, of the one with his right hand, and of the other with his left. And Samson said, Let me die with the Philistines. And he bowed himself with *all his* might; and the house fell upon the lords, and upon all the people that *were* therein." (Jud 16:25-30).

It is interesting to note just how strong the Lord can make a human hand. The above verses say Samson was placed between the two pillars whereupon the house standeth, and that he took hold of these two pillars, one in each hand and bent his body forward from the waist in a bow dislodging the two main house support pillars. Webster's 1828 dictionary defines *hold* as *"to grasp with the hand"* and *bow* as *"to bend or inflect, "to bend the body in token of respect or civility."* These passages make it very clear that Samson stood between two pillars that must have been somewhere between 3 and 6 feet apart, then placing his hands on the backsides of these pillars he bowed forward, stiff armed, and either broke or dislodged both pillars in the direction of his bow.

He did not encircle each column in his arms and squeeze them together nor push them apart laterally, as is usually depicted in "Biblical" cartoons. It is impossible for a hand to grasp a large immovable objects that is being pushed away from the body laterally. The very act of pushing, which is accomplished by the heal of the hand, causes the fingers to fully extend. The act of holding requires the fingers muscles to be in contraction. Samson took hold of the backside of the pillars with some degree of muscle contraction in his fingers, and with stiff arms, fractured them in a forward direction during his bow.

Samson's superhuman hand strength was derived from the infilling of the spirit of the LORD. **"And the spirit of the LORD came mightily upon him, and he rent him [a young lion] as he would have rent a kid, and *he had* nothing in his hand."** (Jud 14:6). Samson was human, Jesus was incarnate deity, He was not mortal nor subject to the filling of the Spirit, hence He had innately greater strength capabilities than even Samson had. Isaiah prophesied, **"Behold, the Lord God will come with a strong hand"** (Isa 40:10) and multiple times God's hands are described as "strong" and "mighty". And, true to prophesy, Jesus came with a strong hand for with strong hands Jesus secured His grasped upon the nails driven through His palms and thereby remained on the cross.

This same hand strength is still exemplified today in the fact that no man is able to pluck a saved person from Jesus' hand; **"I give unto them eternal life; and they shall never perish, neither shall any *man* pluck them out of my hand. My Father, which gave *them* me, is greater than all; and no *man* is able to pluck *them* out of my Father's hand. I and *my* Father are one."** (Jn 10:28-29). For those who doubt, please remember the remark Jesus made to his apostles in Mark 10:27; **"... Jesus looking upon them [the Apostles] saith, With men it is impossible, but not with God: for with God all things are possible"**.

It should never be forgotten that Jesus was God made in the likeness of sinful flesh and God's ways are not man's ways and **"... the wisdom of this world is foolishness with God ..."** (1 Cor 3:19). The LORD has performed numerous medical miracles that skeptics discount today.   God renewed Sarah's womb to fruitfulness, God gave Hezekiah 15 years of additional life when he was sick unto death, and God instantly cleansed Naaman of leprosy, just to name a few.

Thomas said, "**... Except I shall see in his hands the print of the nails, and put my finger into the print of the nails, and thrust my hand into his side, I will not believe.**" Christ replied, "**... Reach hither thy finger, and behold my hands ...**" (Jn 20:27). Jesus was nailed to the cross through His hands, and hands is precisely what is meant. This fact adds yet more proof and substantiates the divinity of Christ because no mortal man could have remained on a crucifix nailed to it as He was. His supernatural grip and supernatural death is the reason the centurion feared greatly, saying, "**... Truly this was the Son of God.**" **(**Matt 27:54).

Lest anyone think that the plan or method of salvation has changed over the course of history it should be noted that in the Old Testament the LORD foreshadowed salvation via a crucified Saviour in approximately 1450 BC when He delivered the Israelites out of Egypt; "**Thou shalt ... well remember what the LORD thy God did unto Pharaoh, and unto all Egypt; the great temptations which thine eyes saw, and the signs, and the wonders, and the mighty hand, and the stretched out arm, whereby the LORD thy God brought thee out:**" (Deut 7:18-19).   One should always remember that Jesus was "**... slain from the foundation of the world.**" (Rev 13:8) and because "**Jesus [is] the same yesterday, and to-day, and for ever.**" (Heb 13:8) the plan and method of salvation has never changed, because it is unchangeable and the good news is, it is still in effect today. Note and note well, **"Salvation *is* of the LORD."** (Jonah 2:9) and only of the LORD. Never forget, **"We are sanctified through the offering of the body of Jesus Christ once *for all.*"** (Heb 10:10).

The LORD's deliverance of the Israelites from Egypt with an outstretched arm foreshadowed that the saving of souls from the damnation of Hell would be via crucifixion of the Saviour. Crucifixion, unknown in Egyptian times, is the only method of public execution that requires that the arms be outstretched. All other forms of public execution (e.g. stoning, sawing asunder, beheading, hanging, burning at the stake, etc.) were performed with the arms restrained at the person's side or behind their back.

Likewise, the LORD also foreshadowed that the Saviour would be able save souls like **"...a brand plucked out of the fire"** (Zech 3:2) due to His mighty hands. The mighty hands of the Son of God grasped the nails driven through His palms and by His own strength and will remained upon the cross. Is it any wonder that **"... the centurion and they that were with him, watching Jesus, and [seeing] the earth quake and [these] things that were done ... feared greatly, [and said] Truly this man was the Son of God."** (Matt 27:54).

The LORD's deliverance of the Israelites from Egypt foreshadowed that the execution of His perfect plan of salvation would be accompanied by the Saviour having to endure great temptations. While Jesus clung to the cross despising the shame, the scribes greatly tempted Jesus to come down from the cross proofing that He is able to save men's souls from the damnation of Hell. Thankfully, He was obedient to His Father unto death; **"Likewise also the chief priests mocking *him*, with the scribes and elders, said, He saved others; himself he cannot save. If he be the King of Israel, let him now come down from the cross, and we will believe him."** (Matt 27:41-42). But **"Be not deceived; God is not mocked: for whatsoever a man soweth, that shall he also reap."** (Gal 6:7) because **"... the LORD God of recompenses shall surely requite."** (Jer 51:56).

    One should note that the great irony is that while the chief priests, scribes and elders thought they had proven Jesus was not the Christ, but when they opened their eyes in the flames of Hell they realized too late that Jesus is indeed exactly who He said He was; the Son of God. And so, it shall be for many, **"...for if ye believe not that I [Jesus] am *he* [the Son of God], ye shall die in your sins."** (Jn 8:24) and **"God shall likewise destroy thee for ever, he shall take thee away, and pluck thee out of *thy* dwelling place, and root thee out of the land of the living. Selah."** (Ps 52:5) because **"... he *is* God, the faithful God, which keepeth covenant and mercy with them that love him and keep his commandments to a thousand generations; and repayeth them that hate him to their face, to destroy them: he will not be slack to him that hateth him, he will repay them to his face."** (Deut 7:9-10) at the Great White Throne Judgement. They, as so many others, learned too late that **"Thou [God], *even* thou, *art* to be feared: and who may stand in thy sight when once thou art angry? Thou didst cause judgment to be**

heard from heaven; the earth feared, and was still, When God arose to judgment, to save all the meek of the earth. Selah." (Ps 76:7-9).

Finally, the LORD's deliverance of the Israelites from Egypt foreshadowed that His perfect plan of salvation would also be accompanied with signs and wonders; **"Now from the sixth hour there was darkness over all the land unto the ninth hour. And about the ninth hour Jesus cried with a loud voice, saying, Eli, Eli, lamasabachthani? That is to say, My God, my God, why hast thou forsaken me? ... Jesus, when he had cried again with a loud voice, yielded up the ghost. And, behold, the veil of the temple was rent in twain from the top to the bottom; and the earth did quake, and the rocks rent; And the graves were opened; and many bodies of the saints which slept arose, And came out of the graves after his resurrection, and went into the holy city, and appeared unto many."** (Matt 27:45-51).

There is no other way to account for the inexplicable extinguishment of the sun for three hours, Jesus crying out with a loud voice moments before He bowed His head and gave up the ghost, the rending of the veil from top to bottom, the world-wide earthquake, the rending of every rock in the world, and the resurrection of many of the saints, than that they were irrefutable God ordained signs and wonders of the first order, as were those performed in Egypt.

"Therefore also now, saith the LORD, turn ye *even* **to me with all your heart, and with fasting, and with weeping, and with mourning: and rend your heart, and not your garments, and turn unto the**

LORD your God: for he *is* gracious and merciful, slow to anger, and of great kindness, and repenteth him of the evil." (Joel 2:12-13). **"And the LORD thy God will circumcise thine heart and the heart of thy seed, to love the LORD thy God with all thine heart, and with all thy soul, that thou mayest live."** (Deut 30:6).

<u>Second Adam</u>

Christ as the second Adam highlights some of what Christ accomplished.

- The first Adam sinned by violating God's Law (civil code). Adam was not deceived, he knew full well that **"... God is not mocked: for whatsoever a man soweth, that shall he also reap."** (Gal. 6:7). Adam also knew that by disobeying God's Law he was going to "know good and evil" because the **"... LORD searcheth all hearts, and understandeth all the imaginations of the thoughts ..."** (1 Chron 28:9).

- The second Adam that took the punishment due the first Adam. The scourging had to be severe because **"... that servant [the first Adam], which knew his lord's will, and prepared not himself, neither did according to his will, shall be beaten with many stripes."** (Lk 12:47) and Lk 24:7 tells us that Jesus said, **"... The Son of man must be delivered into the hands of sinful (i.e. evil) men, and be crucified..."**

- The first Adam agreed to know good and evil at Eve's prompting.

- The second Adam knew evil. Judas Iscariot, the son of perdition, betrayed Jesus into the hands of evil men. We also know without a doubt that it was evil men that scourged Christ, the second Adam, because the law declares; **"Forty stripes he may give him, and not exceed: lest, if he should exceed, and beat him above these with many stripes, then thy brother should seem vile [i.e. evil] unto thee."** (Deut 25:3). It was payment for the first Adam's sin whereby the second Adam reaped the knowledge of evil as no other man has or ever will again.

- The wrath of God was upon the first Adam because **"Thus saith the LORD; Cursed be the man that trusteth in man, and maketh flesh his arm, and whose heart departeth from the LORD."** (Jer 17:5).

- God was well pleased with the second Adam for **"... a voice out of the cloud, ... said, This is my beloved Son, in whom I am well pleased ..."** (Matt 17:5). It was the second Adam **"Who his own self bare our sins in his own body on the tree ..."** (1 Pet 2:24) and removed the first Adam's curse by way of the cross because **"...Cursed is every one that hangeth on a tree."** (Gal 3:10).

- The first Adam caused the earth to be cursed; **"... Because thou hast hearkened unto the voice of thy wife, and hast eaten of the tree, of which I commanded thee, saying Thou shalt not eat of it: cursed is the ground for thy sake; in sorrow** shalt thou eat of it all the days of thy life; Thorns also and thistles shall it bring forth to thee; and thou shalt eat the herb of the field;" (Gen 3: 17-18).

- The second Adam lifted the curse from the earth, for on the cross he wore a crown of thorns; **"And they clothed him with purple, and platted a crown of thorns, and put it about his head,"** (Mk 15:17).

- The first Adam was made a living soul; **"... The first man Adam was made a living soul ..."** (1 Cor 15:45).
- The second Adam was made a quickening spirit; **"... the last [second] Adam was made a quickening spirit."** (1 Cor 15:45).

- The first Adam was flesh made sinful.
- The second Adam was made in the likeness of sinful flesh. His scourged body was hung upon a tree as a testimony to the whole world that willful flesh that **"... plowed wickedness ... [will]reap iniquity [because it] hath eaten the fruit of lies: ..."** (Hos 10:13).

- The first Adam was sinful flesh.
- The second Adam showed the world that sinful flesh **"... is sown in corruption; it is raised in incorruption: It is sown in dishonour; it is raised in glory: it is sown in weakness; it is raised in power:"** (1 Cor 15:42-43).

- The first Adam was a sinner; **"If we say that we have no sin, we deceive ourselves, and the truth is not in us."** (1 Jn 1:8).
- The second Adam was sinless; **"And ye know that he [Jesus] was manifested to take away ours sins; and in him is no sin."** (1 Jn 3:5).

- The first Adam ate of the cursed earth all the days of his life because **"... cursed is the ground for thy sake; in sorrow shalt thou eat of it all the days of thy life;"** (Gen 3:17).
- The second Adam informs us that our immortal bodies will feast on manna and God's Word. **"... Man shall not live by bread alone, but by every word that proceedeth out of the mouth of God."** (Matt 4:4). **"Our fathers did eat manna in the desert; as it is written, He gave them bread from heaven to eat"** (Jn 6:31).

- The first Adam was mortal. **"It is sown a natural body; it is raised a spiritual body. There is a natural body, and there is a spiritual body."** (1 Cor 15:44). **"And all the days that Adam lived were nine hundred and thirty years: and he died"** (Gen 5:5).
- The second Adam is immortal. **"... I [Jesus] lay down my life, that I might take it again. No man taketh it from me, but I lay it down of myself. I have power to lay it down, and I have power to take it again."** (Jn 10:17-18).

- The first Adam lived and died on the earth. "**...
  LORD God formed man of the dust of the
  ground, and breathed into his nostrils the
  breath of life; and man became a living soul.**"
  (Gen 2:7), "**And all the days that Adam lived
  were nine hundred and thirty years: and he
  died.**" (Gen 5:5).
- The second Adam, the Lord Jesus Christ, came
  from the 3rd heaven and died in 1st heaven (lifted
  off the earth via the cross) paying for the sin of
  the world. "**Howbeit that was not first which
  is spiritual, but that which is natural; and
  afterward that which is spiritual. The first
  man is of the earth, earthy: the second man is
  the Lord from heaven. As is the earthy, such
  are they also that are earthy: and as is the
  heavenly, such are they also that are heavenly.
  And as we have born the image of the earthy,
  we shall also bear the image of the heavenly.**"
  (1 Cor 15:46- 49).

- The first Adam's body contained blood; "**... the
  voice of thy brother's blood crieth unto me
  [God] from the ground.**" (Gen 4:10).
- The second Adam's glorified body is bloodless;
  "**Then saith he [Jesus] to Thomas, Reach hither
  thy finger, and behold my hands; and reach
  hither thy hand, and thrust it into my side: and
  be not faithless, but believing.**" (Jn 20:27).

And so, by the second Adam, the life that is in the
blood was vanquished. By way of the scourging and

crucifixion, the Lord Jesus Christ, the second Adam, openly (**"... for this thing was not done in a corner"** Acts 26:26) proved to the world that **"... the weakness of God is stronger than men"** (1 Cor 1:25) and **"... no flesh should glory in His presence"** (1 Cor 1:29), for in the flesh **"... dwelleth no good thing: for to will is present ..."** (Rom 7:18).

The second Adam suffered so as to present a graphic visual that men should fear the LORD and work out their own salvation with fear and trembling. It was a vivid, bloody reminder that **"The fear of the LORD *is* a fountain of life, to depart from the snares of death."** (Prove. 14:27). Isaiah said it best in Chapter 45 and verse 9: **"Woe unto him that striveth with his maker! ..."** Job 19:20 reminds us that even the best escape only by the skin of their teeth from the righteous judgment of God. And for the benefit of the unrepentant and unbelieving, who **"... seeing see not; and hearing they hear not, neither do they understand"** (Matt 13:14), the scourging and crucifixion serves as the final visual testimony of God's warning to **"Be ye afraid of the sword [the military and judicial arms of Government]: for wrath *bringeth* the punishments of the sword, that ye may know *there is* a judgement"** (Job 19:29) and to **"... Be not afraid of them that kill the body, and after that, have no more that they can do. ... [but to] Fear him, which after he hath killed, hath power to cast into hell ..."** (Lk 12:4-5). All now are all without excuse because the second Adam, the Lord Jesus Christ; **"... now once in the end of the world hath he appeared to put away sin by the sacrifice of himself. And as it is appointed unto men once to die,**

but after this the judgment." (Heb 9:26-27).

The second Adam was truly victorious in every point where the first Adam failed. It was through the bloody crucifixion that Christ proved to the unbelieving that **"... greater is he that is in you, than he that is in the world"** (1 Jn 4:4) and **"It is the spirit that quickeneth; the flesh profiteth nothing ..."** (Jn 6:63).

Blood And Water Witness

"And at the ninth hour Jesus cried with a loud voice, saying, Eloi, Eloi, lama sabachthani? which is, being interpreted, My God, my God, why hast thou forsaken me?" (Mk 15:34). **"And Jesus cried with a loud voice, and gave up the ghost."** (Mk 15:37). **"And when the centurion, which stood over against him saw that he so cried out, and gave up the ghost, he said, Truly this man was the Son of God."** (Mk 15:39). **"The Jews therefore, because it was the preparation, that the bodies should not remain upon the cross on the sabbath day, (for that sabbath day was an high day,) besought Pilate that their legs might be broken, and *that* they might be taken away. Then came the soldiers, and brake the legs of the first, and of the other which was crucified with him. But when they came to Jesus, and saw that he was dead already, they brake not his legs: But one of the soldiers with a spear pierced his side, and forth with came there out blood and water. And he that saw *it* bare record, and his record is true; and he knoweth that he saith true, that ye might believe. For these things were done, that the scripture should be fulfilled, A bone of him shall not be broken. And again another scripture**

saith, They shall look on him whom they pierced."
(Jn 19:31-37).

John bare record of the discharge of blood followed by water that you might believe. A *record* or *testimony* is *a solemn declaration or affirmation made for the purpose of establishing or proving some fact.* John further declares, his testimony is absolutely true and God knows that he is speaking the truth. He emphatically declares that he saw what he claims he saw, and what he saw, he accurately recorded. The practical utility of his testimony should be **"... that ye might believe ..."**

What John observed was real and infallible proof that Jesus is truly the Christ, the Son of God. Consequently, John's testimony of his witnessing the effluence of blood and water is to further persuade us to believe the truth of the gospel. In other words, that ye might believe that Jesus is the Christ, the Son of God. Believing Jesus is the Son of God, is absolutely essential, because it is only by **"... believing ye might have life through his name."** (Jn 20:31).

John 19:34 states that from His pierced side **"... came out blood and water."** Skeptics point out that such a thing is an utter impossibility, and for that reason, they refused to believe John's testimony. Others propose that the blood and water discharge was just John's way of saying that the foundation of the church had just been laid. This explanation does not address the observed facts nor explain how such a phenomena could happen.

Still others propose that the physical cause of death was a ruptured heart, caused by the great mental suffering He endured. The ruptured heart filled the pericardium (the lining that surrounds the heart) with a large volume of blood. This blood subsequently decomposed and when the pericardium was pierced by the Roman soldier's spear, out flowed a stream of clear watery liquid, intermixed with clotted blood.

While this is a touching theory it is not supported by history, physiology, nor Scripture. If the pericardium filled with blood and the Roman spear punctured it, the blood would have filled the punctured lung vice flowing out of the body because Roman spears did not have blood gutters. A spear tip with a blood gutter might have provided a channel for the blood to exit the body, however such design features were not incorporated into Roman armament.

This theory also fails from a physiological aspect as well. John did not attest to seeing a blood and water mixture. He did not see water intermixed with blood clots, he saw blood exit first followed by water and Jesus did not remain on the cross long enough for His blood to decompose and fractionate into its primary components, i.e. blood and plasma.

Finally, this theory is inconsistent with Scripture. Psalms 16:10 says **"...neither wilt thou [God] suffer thine Holy One to see corruption"** therefore decomposed blood as the source of blood and water is not a viable explanation for John's observation. Furthermore, it should be noted that it was impossible for Jesus to have died from a ruptured heart because **"... the weakness of God is stronger than men."** (1 Cor 1:25).

If however, one considers John's testimony in the light of modern medical knowledge, one is able to see what a strong testimony the blood and water effluence really makes. John's record confirms that Jesus was indeed the Christ, the Son of God. John's testimony proves beyond a shadow of a doubt that He was truly made sin for us and that He did bear that fearful load of sin personally. It verifies that God the Father placed the sin of the world upon His Son, and because the Father is too holy to look upon sin with any degree of allowance, turned from His Son in those last moments, bringing forth Jesus' cry of despair: **"My God, my God, why hast thou forsaken me? ..."**

The scourging that Jesus received resulted in pleural effusion (bloody fluid build-up between the ribs and lungs in the pleural cavity). Christ was subsequently crucified and while hanging on the cross He was **"... made to be sin for us who knew no sin; that we might be made the righteousness of God in him."** (2 Cor 5:21) during the time when **"... from the sixth hour there was darkness over all the land unto the ninth hour."** Between the sixth and ninth hour Christ bore our sins and paid our sin debt. The physical manifestation of this was, sin entered into Christ's red blood cells. Christ's blood became sinful bearing mans sin; **"Who his own self bare our sins in his own body on the tree, that we, being dead to sins, should live unto righteousness: by whose stripes ye were healed."** (1 Pet 2:24).

At the ninth hour, Christ having been **"... made to be sin for us who knew no sin..."** (2 Cor 5:21) completed His mission on the cross. He had successfully taken **"... away the sin of the world"** (Jn 1:29) by taking it upon Himself. With His divine mission accomplished, He **"... gave up the ghost."** for; **"... I [Jesus] lay down**

**my life, that I might take it again. No man taketh it
from me, but I lay it down of myself. I have power
to lay it down, and I have power to take it again.
This commandment have I received of my Father."**
(Jn 10:17-18).

The Bible very clearly states in 1 Peter 2:24 that
Jesus **"Who his own self bare our sins in his own body
on the tree ..."** Consequently, as a result of this divine
act the pure, sinless blood that flowed within Jesus
became sinful. The antibodies in His blood plasma
detected the new, foreign element of sin in His red blood
cells and triggered an immune reaction whereby His
blood agglutinated. The agglutinated red blood cells
then settled to the bottom of the pleural effusion due to
their greater specific gravity.

When the soldier, who had been sent to break the
victim's legs and thereby hastening their death, noted
that Jesus was already dead, he thrust his spear into His
side just to verify the fact that Jesus had indeed expired.
The spear punctured the pleural effusion, which resulted
in the effluence of blood and water. The discharge from
the pleural effusion consisted of agglutinated red blood
cells followed by the clear plasma, that was referred to
as water. Such a discharge of blood and water from
the pleural effusion would be very distinctive and
discernable, and correspond exactly with what the
Apostle John attested to.

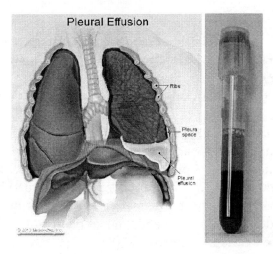

Agglutinated Blood

Jesus' pleural effusion discharge, with its two separate and distinct components, namely blood followed by water, provides yet another infallible proof that Jesus was truly the Son of God, very God and very man, made **"... in the likeness of sinful ..."** flesh yet without sin. A pleural effusion discharge from an ordinary mortal man would have been nothing more than a light red, watery flux. Consequently, as John points out, it is yet another infallible proof provided by God **"... that ye might believe."**

Blood flowed from Christ's body first because payment of sin must precede salvation. Water followed the blood as proof positive that Jesus Christ has the ability to provide us the new birth as a spiritual man. Jesus stated it this way; **"... Verily, verily, I say unto thee, Except a man be born of water and *of* the Spirit, he cannot enter into the kingdom of God."**

(Jn 3:5). Also, water followed the blood as a graphic and literal fulfillment of scripture; **"... as the scripture hath said, out of His [Jesus'] belly shall flow rivers of living water."** (Jn 7:38).

The LORD God opened the first Adam's (natural man's) side thereby providing us the means (Eve) for our first (natural) birth. Natural man opened the Second Adam's (Lord Jesus Christ's) side, in the very same location, thereby providing us the means, (**"... born of water ..."** (Jn 3:5)), for our second (spiritual) birth. It was because of this divine act **"... we live unto the Lord ..."** (Rom 14:8) and **"for ... [you] to live [as a redeemed soul]** *is* **Christ ..."** (Phil 1:21). **"... The first man Adam was made a living soul; the last Adam** *was made* **a quickening spirit. Howbeit that** *was* **not first which is spiritual, but that which is natural; and afterward that which is spiritual."** (1 Cor 15:45-46).

It is also interesting to note that, guided by the hand of Providence, the Roman soldier pierced Jesus' side in the exact same location that God pierced Adam's side for the removal of the rib He used to create Eve, the **"... mother of all living."** (Gen 3:20). The first Adam was operated upon by the LORD God who removed 1 pair of ribs which He used to create Eve; **"And the LORD god caused a deep sleep to fall upon Adam, and he slept: and he took one of his ribs, and closed up the flesh instead thereof; And the rib, which the LORD God had taken from man, made he a woman, and brought her unto the man."** (Gen 2:21-22).

Rib cages serve to protect the heart. By God's operation Adam's original 13 pair of ribs was reduced to 12 pair of ribs. This is very significant when you consider that bovine (e.g. the bullock required for the sin-offering, the golden calf, the fire-god Molech) and swine (i.e. the abomination that maketh desolate) have 13 pair of ribs. Biblically the number 13 represents rebellion, apostasy, defection, corruption, disintegration, or some other kindred idea and bulls represent wicked, violent and furious enemies of the Lord as stated in Job 22:12, **"Many bulls have compassed me: strong *bulls* of Bashan have beset me round…"**

Thanks to God's intervention however, man has 12 pair of ribs today. The number 12 biblically signifies perfection of government, i.e. God's civil code. Therefore it can be stated that mans heart is made to be protected by God's perfect civil code. Said another way, it is by obeying God's civil code that man is protected from sin. But because man is incapable of perfectly obeying God's civil code, one must be in Christ to receive the protection the heart needs from sin. It is His 12 pair of ribs that keep your heart safe. Paul the Apostle explains it this way; **"For as many of you as have been baptized into Christ have put on Christ."** (Gal 3:27). He is your breast plate of righteousness that deflect the fiery darts of the Devil.

While on the subject of ribs, it is also interesting to point out that Jesus is called the Lamb of God. Lambs have 14 pair of ribs. The number 14 Biblically represents double 7 which in turn represents supreme spiritual perfection and Jesus without a doubt, is spiritual perfection personified for the Bible says; **"He *is* the Rock, his work *is* perfect: for all his ways *are* judgment: a God of truth and without iniquity, just and right *is* he."** (Deut 32:4).

Fulfilled prophetic events such as this one should convince all to put their full trust and confidence in the Bible. This event should crystallize every person's faith thereby allowing all to say; **"I know that, whatsoever God doeth, it shall be for ever: nothing can be put to it, nor any thing taken from it: and God doeth *it*, that *men* should fear before him."** (Ecc 3:14). Based upon this witnessed event, all should now fully believe that God is truly able to save your soul from the damnation of Hell as promised.

Finally, John's eyewitness account of the fulfillment of scripture is yet another indisputable validation of God's righteousness. God as portrayed to man in the King James Bible is The Sovereign God and this is why what Balaam said to Balak is the truth, the whole truth, and nothing but the truth. **"God *is* not a man, that he should lie; neither the son of man, that he should repent: hath he said, and shall he not do *it*? or hath he spoken, and shall he not make it good?"** (Num 23:19).

Blood Of The New Testament
"And as they did eat, Jesus took bread, and blessed, and brake *it*, and gave to them, and said, Take, eat: this is my body. And he took the cup, and when he had given thanks, he gave it to them: and they all drank of it. And he said unto them, This is my blood of the new testament, which is shed for many." (Mk 14:22-24).

The Lord left us with a symbolic method of instruction to remind us of what our Saviour's blood accomplished for us. **"... the *same* night on which he was betrayed, he took bread, and when he had given**

thanks he brake *it* **and said, Take, eat; this is my body which is broken for you: this do in remembrance of me. After the same manner also** *he took* **the cup, when he had supped, saying, This cup is the New Testament in my blood: this do ye, as oft as ye drink** *it***, in remembrance of me. For as often as ye eat this bread and drink this cup, ye do show the Lord's death till he come."** (1 Cor 11:23-26).

Jesus teaches us very plainly that the primary object of the Lord's Supper is symbolic and commemorative. It is designed to keep us ever aware of the fact that Jesus Christ shed His blood for the remission of our sins according to the Scriptures.

The Lord's Supper presents an analogy between the wants of the body and wants of the soul. It emphasizes that just having our physical needs met is not enough. We must never forget how our true need was met; Christ shed his blood for the remission of our sins. The broken bread represents Christ who willingly let His body be broken in order that we might have an immortal body. The new wine represents the blood of Christ because only the shed blood of Christ can quench our thirst for eternal life.

Bloody Return

"The LORD is a man of war:" (Ex 15:3) and forewarns us of the certain doom that awaits all unbelievers at Christ's return; **"For, behold, the LORD will come with fire, and with his chariots like a whirlwind, to render his anger with fury, and his rebuke with flames of fire. For by fire and by his sword will the LORD plead with all flesh: and the**

slain of the LORD shall be many. They that sanctify themselves, and purify themselves in the gardens behind one *tree* in the midst, eating swine's flesh, and the abomination, and the mouse, shall be consumed together, saith the LORD. For I *know* their works and their thoughts ..." (Isa 66:15-18).

The Lord Jesus Christ will "... tread them in mine anger, and trample them in my fury; and their blood shall be sprinkled upon my garments, and I will stain all my raiment. For the day of vengeance *is* in mine heart, and the year of my redeemed is come." (Isa 63:3-4).

At Jesus Christ's return there will be the greatest blood bath that the world has ever seen. The Revelation of Jesus Christ to St. John informs us that at the Battle of Armageddon He will slaughter the 200 million strong army of the antichrist for they are "... fearful, unbelieving, abominable, murderers, whoremongers, sorcerers, idolaters, and liars, [that] shall have their part in the lake which burneth with fire and brimstone: which is the second death." (Rev 21:8). "... the loftiness [self-righteousness] of man shall be bowed down, and the haughtiness of men shall be made low: and the LORD alone shall be exalted in that day. And the idols he [the LORD] shall utterly abolish. And they shall go into the holes of the rocks, and into the caves of the earth, for fear of the LORD, and for the glory of his majesty, when he ariseth to shake terribly the earth." (Amos 2:17-19).

By the end of the battle a literal river shall have formed in the Valley of Megiddo from the blood of the damned souls that were slain in the battle. Based upon the geography where the battle will be fought and the volume of human bloodshed during the slaughter (approximately 435 million gallons), a river of human blood will flow that will be 12 feet wide, 4 feet deep and 176 miles long.

After the battle, Jesus Christ shall lead His victorious army home. The procession of battle weary saints, all riding on white steeds, shall wade across this river of human blood on their way home to Jerusalem; **"And I saw heaven opened, and behold a white horse; and he that sat upon him *was* called Faithful and True, and in righteousness he doth judge and make war. His eyes *were* as a flame of fire, and on his head *were* many crown; and he had a name written, that no man knew, but he himself. And he *was* clothed with a vesture dipped in blood: and his name is called The Word of God. And the armies *which were* in heaven followed him upon white horses, clothed in fine linen, white and clean. And out of his mouth goeth a sharp sword, that with it he should smite the nations: and he shall rule them with a rod of iron: and he treadeth the winepress of the fierceness and wrath of Almighty God. "And he hath on *his* vesture and on his thigh a name written, KING OF KINGS, AND LORD OF LORDS."** (Rev 19:11-16).

Power Of Christ's Blood

Christ's blood is more precious than gold or silver; **"Forasmuch as ye know that ye were not redeemed with corruptible things, *as* silver and gold, form your vain conversation *received* by tradition from your fathers; but with the precious blood of Christ, as of a**

lamb without blemish and without spot:" (1 Pet 1:18-19).

Man values two metals, silver and gold as most precious and has made them earth's standards of value and medium of exchange, yet for our redemption God calls them only corruptible things compared to the blood of Christ. Our redemption was purchased with something exceedingly more precious and powerful than earth's most precious materials, God's one and only begotten Son's blood.

- *Christ's blood frees us from mans false doctrine*
  "... ye were not redeemed with corruptible things, ... from your vain conversation received by tradition from your fathers; But with the precious blood of Christ, ..." (1 Pet 1:18-19).

- *Christ's blood purges our conscience*
  "How much more shall the blood of Christ, ... purge your conscience from dead works to serve the living God? " (Heb 9:14).

- *Christ's blood provides forgiveness of sins*
  "... we have redemption through his blood, even the forgiveness of sins" (Col 1:14).

- *Christ's blood cleanses us from all sin*
  "... the blood of Jesus Christ his Son cleanseth us from all sin." (1 Jn 1:7).

- *Christ's blood justifies us before a Holy God*
  "... being now justified by his blood, we shall be saved from wrath through him." (Rom 5:9).

- *Christ's blood redeems us from the law of sin and death*
  "...Thou [Jesus] ... hast redeemed us to God by thy blood ..." (Rev 5:9).

- *Christ's blood makes us righteous*
  "... **Being justified [made righteous] freely by his grace through the redemption that is in Christ Jesus: Whom God hath set forth to be a propitiation through faith in his blood, ...**" (Rom 3:20).
- *Christ's blood sanctifies us*
  "**Wherefore Jesus also, that he might sanctify the people with his own blood, suffered without the gate**" (Heb 13:12).
- *Christ's blood brings us close to God*
  "... **ye who sometimes were far off are made nigh by the blood of Christ.**" (Eph 2:13).
- *Christ's blood gives us peace with God*
  "**Therefore being justified by faith, we have peace with God through our Lord Jesus Christ:**" (Rom 5:1).
- *Christ's blood sanctifies the Holy Spirit to us*
  "**Elect according to the foreknowledge of God the Father, through sanctification of the Spirit, unto obedience and sprinkling of the blood of Jesus Christ: Grace unto you, and peace, be multiplied.**" (1 Pet 1:2).
- *Christ's blood seals us into the New Covenant of grace*
  "... **A new covenant, he [Jesus] hast made the first old...**" (Heb 8:13). "**And to Jesus the mediator of the new covenant, and to the blood of sprinkling, that speaketh better things than that of Abel.**" (Heb 13:24).
- *Christ's blood gives us spiritual boldness*
  "**Having therefore, brethren, boldness to enter

into the holiest by the blood of Jesus," (Heb 10:19).

- *Christ's blood gives us the power to overcome the Satan*
  "… they overcame him [Satan] by the blood of the Lamb, and by the word of their testimony; …" (Rev 12:11).
- *Christ's blood gives us immortality*
  "Whoso eateth my flesh, and drinketh my blood, hath eternal life; and I will raise him up at the last day." (Jn 6:54).
- *Christ's blood reconciles all things unto Himself*
  "… having made peace through the blood of his cross, by him to reconcile all things unto himself; by him, I say, whether they be things in earth, or things in heaven." (Col 1:20)

Washed In The Blood

It is very important to notice that the very first step in obtaining victory over death and Hell is to be "born of God". The Bible is emphatic; "Ye must be born again". It is also clear that it is our faith in the power of Christ's blood that gives us the victory that overcomes the world. When we get washed in the blood of Christ, God likens our sin removal to twenty worldly concepts in order we can better understand just how completely the cleansing process is;

1. They are blotted out   (Isa 43:25)
2. They are borne away by another   (1 Pet 2:24)
3. They are cast behind God's back   (Isa 38:17)
4. They are cast into the depths of the sea (Mic 7:19)
5. They are washed away   (1 Jn 1:7)

6. They are covered   (Rom 4:7)
7. They are finished   (Dan 9:24)
8. They are forgiven   (Col 2:13)
9. They are not beheld   (Num 23:21)
10. They are not imputed   (Rom 4:8)
11. They are not remembered   (Heb 8:12)
12. They are pardoned   (Mic 7:18)
13. They are passed away   (Zech 3:4)
14. They are purged   (Heb 1:3)
15. They are put away   (Heb 9:26)
16. They are remitted   (Acts 10:43)
17. They are removed   (Psm 103:12)
18. They are subdued   (Mic 7:19)
19. They are sought for and not found   (Jer 1:20)
20. They are taken away   (Isa 6:7)

<u>Blood Refused</u>

It is essential that you fully understand that Jesus is God, He is one with the Father, that He is truly the Son of God, and that only His blood is able to wash our sins away and make us righteous. If you die, in your sins, never having repented and accepting the Lord Jesus Christ as your Saviour, you are in fact stating that you are not a sinner because;

- Your good works outweighed your bad
- You kept the Law
- You were religious and sincerely and faithfully worshiped a god whom you thought to be God

and therefore not the least bit apprehensive about falling into the hands of the living God.

Even if this were true, which it certainly is not for; **"...** *there is* **not a just man upon earth, that doeth**

good, and sinneth not." (Ecc 7:20) you would still be brought before the Great White Throne Judgement for committing the following capital offenses;

1. Calling God a liar
2. Unbelief in Jesus Christ
3. Denying the Holiness of Christ's blood

The proceedings would go something like this;

Charge # 1:   Calling God a liar
No matter what you might say, the King James Bible testifies; **"God ...cannot lie, ..."** (Titus 1:2) and **"... he that believeth not God hath made him a liar; because he believeth not the record that God gave of his Son."** (1 Jn 5:10).

Charge # 2:   Unbelief in Jesus Christ
No matter what you might say, the King James Bible testifies; **"... he that believeth not is condemned already, because he hath not believed in the name of the only begotten Son of God."** (Jn 3:18).

Charge # 3:   Denying the Holiness of Christ's blood
No matter what you might say, the King James Bible testifies; **"He that despised Moses' law died without mercy under two or three witnesses: Of how much sorer punishment, suppose ye, shall he be thought worthy, who hath trodden under foot the Son of God, and hath counted the blood of the covenant, wherewith he was sanctified, an unholy thing, ..."** (Heb 10:28-29).

The verdict: **GUILTY!   GUILTY!   GUILTY!**

Your sentence: **ETERNAL DAMNATION!**

Do not forget, the decision is final. The decision is incontestable. There is no one to whom you may appeal. God Himself clearly told you, **"...I *am* the first, and I *am* the last; and beside me *there is* no God."** (Is 44:6).

God's mighty angels will straightway cast your self-righteous body and soul, into the flaming lake without water that burns with brimstone. There will be no one to blame but yourself. Remember, you, a free moral agent, knowingly and willingly chose to reject the truth that, **"... *there is* one God, and one mediator between God and men, the man Christ Jesus"** (1 Tim 2:5).

Conclusion

Christ shed His blood on the cross of Calvary 2011 years ago. When Jesus said, **"It is finished"** (Jn 19:30), He bowed His head and gave up the Ghost. He announced to the world that His self-sacrifice was completed and that all the requirements of the law had been duly kept in their entirety.

Consequently, our hope of salvation from the wrath of God and resurrection from the dead can only be realized through a personal and individual acceptance of the atoning blood of Christ. To reject it, or neglect it, seals your eternal doom. **"...for there is none other name under heaven given among men, whereby we must be saved."** (Acts 4:12).

If you do not believe in redemption and salvation through the shed blood of Jesus Christ, you do not believe God. Therefore, take heed before it is eternally too late. Be sure you are indeed; **"Elect according to the foreknowledge of God the Father, through sanctification of the Spirit unto obedience and sprinkling of the blood of Jesus Christ ..."** (1 Pet 1:2).

Knowing that you **"... have redemption through his blood, even the forgiveness of sins, according to the riches of his [God's] grace;"** (Eph 1:7). **"And, having made peace through the blood of his cross ..."** (Col 1:20). **"... we shall be saved from wrath through him."** (Rom 5:9). **"For whatsoever is born of God overcometh the world: and this is the victory that overcometh the world, *even* our faith."** (1 Jn 5:4-5).

So do not be deceived because **"Neither is there salvation in any other: for there is none other name under heaven given among men, whereby we must be saved."** (Acts 4:12).

And All The People Said, Amen and Amen!

Afterword

You've just read the old, old story, how a Saviour came from Glory. How He gave His life on Calvary to save a wretch like me. You read about His groaning, of His precious blood's atoning. Have you repented of your sins and won the victory?

If not, be sure you ask yourself this question before your eyes close in death; **"How shall [I] escape [the damnation of Hell] if [I] neglect so great salvation; which at the first began to be spoken by the Lord, and was confirmed unto us by them that heard him; God also bearing them witness, both with signs and wonders, and with divers miracles, and gifts of the Holy Ghost, according to his own will?"** (Heb 2:3-4)